Turn Over the Rock

Discovering Opportunity, Finding Grace,
and Getting Clients

TYSON KNAUF

Turn Over the Rock

Copyright © 2024, Tyson Knauf

Published by:
Thought Leader Press
New York / Oklahoma

Hardcover 978-1-61343-156-6

Paperback 978-1-61343-157-3

E-book 978-1-61343-158-0

Table of Contents

Introduction 6

Why Turn Over the Rock? 17

Chapter 1: Wild Quail 22

Observe Them 34

Seek to Understand 36

Something to Perch On 37

Guide Them 40

Let Them Fly Away 41

Chapter 2: Snakes 46

Acknowledging Your State 67

Probe Yourself 69

Move Forward 70

Find New Stimuli 72

Pique Your Curiosity 74

Chapter 3: Spiders 78

Hope in the Process 97

Surround Yourself with the Right People 100

Vulnerable Enough to Help 102

Chapter 4: Ant Bully 108

Pain Sparks Empathy and Connection 116

Discovering Life Through Pain 118

Empathizing with Life 122
Cross-Pollination of Intelligence 124
Relating to Behavior 126

Chapter 5: Stick Bugs...................... 132

Spread Like Wildfire........................... 138
Look Like a Branch............................ 144
Like Johnny Appleseed........................ 150
Engage Like a Chameleon..................... 153

Chapter 6: Bees............................. 158

Feed Them 171
Monitor Them 174
Give Them Space to Grow 177
Extract the Honey............................ 180
Take the Gloves Off 182

Chapter 7: People 190

Find Your Mentor 198
Listen 202
Open Mind 205
Work Through Doubt and Fear................ 209
Act in Faith 212

Conclusion 222

Introduction

I n a society that often values conformity over exploration and curiosity, it can be easy to lose sight of our
true selves.

As someone who has spent years in the banking industry,
I understand the pitfalls of being consumed by the daily
grind and forgetting about the questions that matter.

But my childhood taught me the joy that comes from
uncovering the unknown, which has become the cor-
nerstone of my personal and professional life. I have
embraced the art of exploration to expand my network
and cultivate a better understanding of myself and others.

Throughout our lives, we are bound to face situations that
threaten our sense of identity and self-acceptance. These
encounters can be critical junctures that mold our view-
points and stoke our interests. I encountered one such
experience during my early days in the banking industry.

During a team party get-together, we were all exchanging cards. I got my card that featured a band of horse-riding cowboys donning classic cowboy hats. The center cowboy was wearing a flamingo hat and stood out among the others.

I could have taken offense, but the card carried a message that said something like, "There's an odd one in all of us, and we love you for it," and I immediately understood the spirit in which it was given. It was a great compliment and at that moment, I felt proud to be different.

These kinds of experiences gave me greater enthusiasm to pursue my interests, no matter how peculiar they might be. In life, we frequently encounter criticism and the pressure to fit in, and it is so easy to become mired in conventional norms and neglect our unique abilities and distinctive passions.

My pursuit of grace has enabled me to approach life with a more relaxed mindset, relieving pressures from a society that sometimes sets unreasonable expectations and allowing me to enjoy the process of my personal growth with a sense of ease and enjoyment.

I realized my superpower lies in my ability to laugh at myself and the ability to find humor in what I do without feeling offended. This ability to laugh at ourselves, let go of unnecessary pressures, and embrace grace in our encounters is something we can all benefit from.

Relying on grace helped me cultivate this mindset. There is more grace in the world than we frequently realize, and I think that deliberately seeking it is an essential part of life. It unlocks a more harmonious and joyous existence, free from the weight of perfectionism and self-doubt.

Unfortunately, I don't think many people actively seek out and pursue grace. Instead, we frequently chase perfection in everything and then forget to extend grace to ourselves and others when things don't go as we planned.

I have always been fascinated by bugs and insects since I was a child. I would spend countless hours observing ants on a sidewalk or on the driveway in front of my parents' house.

One of the fondest recollections I have from when I was young, is of the edge of the road of our house, where a massive and oddly-formed rock hedge stood.

The rocks were large, almost boulder-sized, but were still small enough for me to lift. I would excitedly turn over each rock to see what spiders and bugs were hiding underneath them. Although I usually found spiders, I was always curious about what I would see next.

To this day, I continue to be fascinated by insects, spiders, reptiles, and all other critters. This curiosity has followed me everywhere. For instance, during my first trip to a jungle in Costa Rica back in 2007, all I wanted to do was flip over rocks and go far into the forest to explore and discover new things.

My entire life has been consumed by this spirit of exploration, primarily because I get bored quickly, and therefore need to constantly discover and learn new things.

I started my profession in banking six years ago, but I found it rather boring and monotonous for my taste. My primary goal at the time was to get into the business sector, but I didn't really have a clear plan. So I had decided to start with business banking.

During my time in that role, I realized how different I was from my colleagues. While that was perfectly acceptable, I learned that my genuine enjoyment and passion in life was really about exploring and uncovering new things, similar to what I loved doing when I was a child.

As I was looking for ways to pursue my passion for discovering new things and turning over rocks, I ended up branching out and going out into consulting.

I took a course and learned how to build networks on LinkedIn, which I found to be a neat platform at the time. I didn't know how to use it, so I paid someone to teach me.

From there, I started reaching out to people, figuring out what was going on in their lives, and offering to help. That's how it started for me.

I was still working as a banker, but I found that I really enjoyed the process of reaching out to people and telling them what I had learned about LinkedIn in my spare time.

It started when I helped a friend and then that friend's friend, and soon I was reaching out to more people, sharing some insights, learning a bit about their lives and their businesses and what they wanted to accomplish.

To me, the joy in discovery comes from changing our perspective on a person or situation. Too often, we think we know everything until we turn them over like a rock and discover something completely different.

The truth is that we live in a big and largely unexplored universe. This is what motivates me to keep exploring my surroundings.

I also find joy in introducing others to new experiences and discoveries. When I was in Costa Rica, I was with a friend who had lived there for five years selling real estate. We visited Whale Tail Beach, just north of the Osa Peninsula, where during a low tide, the beach looks like a whale's tail.

As we combed the beach, I flipped over a rock and found a brittle star. Unlike starfish that move so slowly it's hard to tell if they're alive or not, brittle stars move quickly and resemble a creature straight out of a science fiction book.

My friend was so surprised and said, "I have been here for five years, and I've never seen one of those; how did you find that?" But it was simply a matter of turning over a rock, and there it was, an incredible creature just tucked away.

My passion to discover and explore new things extends to reptiles as well. I have a couple of snakes, and my wife is not always thrilled when I show them to guests. Anytime someone new comes over, I can't help but manage to steer the conversation toward these snakes.

Some people are hesitant to see them, and some are scared, but for those who are curious, I find it rewarding to teach them a thing or two about snakes. If they can leave with an appreciation for the creatures that they didn't have before, no matter how small, I consider it a success.

I believe this passion for sharing what I love is something we all have in common to some extent. However, we sometimes struggle with how to communicate things effectively or fear that others won't appreciate what we enjoy. To me, however, it is worth taking that risk.

Over the years, I have become a collector of reptiles, spiders, and insects. I am now at a stage where I have two snakes, several tarantulas, and a host of other creatures.

Interestingly, when I was young, my mom would always say, "You can have anything, but you can't have snakes and rodents." So I found solace in collecting exotic insects like praying mantises, leaf bugs, stick bugs, and giant African and American millipedes.

I vividly recall buying a giant African millipede at the West Edmonton Mall when I was eight or nine, and it was one of the most exciting things I have ever bought.

It all started when I found out that my brother's biology teacher had a pet stick bug, and it piqued my interest. I had no idea I could acquire insects that weren't native to my area.

My curiosity led me to the internet of the early 2000s, where I discovered that you could purchase bugs online. Soon after that, I began collecting bugs myself.

During a walk home from the bus with a fellow student who was my sister's age, he pointed out some bug that he knew. Intrigued by my fascination with insects, he shared his own interest in the subject.

I invited him to see my collection, and he ended up purchasing a giant Vietnamese centipede for himself. I was thrilled to know someone that shared my own interests.

Eventually, I had to give up my bug collection when I traveled to Germany for a couple of years as a church missionary. When I returned home and met my wife, I didn't have any bugs, which she appreciated. And now, with my growing collection, she jokes, "You pulled the wool over my eyes." But even she has since developed an appreciation for my bug collection.

A few years into our marriage, a friend and coworker at the bank had to find a new home for her son's chameleon, a creature that I had always wanted.

After some convincing, my wife agreed to take the chameleon in. But the task of feeding it posed a challenge because chameleons eat bugs. So I decided to start a cockroach colony because they were cheaper to maintain than crickets.

When we moved into our first house five years later, my chameleon had passed away. But by then, I wanted a snake, because I had always wanted to have one.

A few months before moving into our new home, I got my Dumeril's Boa, who has become like a good friend of the family. He is like a lap snake who hangs out with us as we watch movies.

Though my passion for snakes, insects, and other seemingly strange creatures is not the norm, I've embraced it.

Sometimes we have interests that may seem unconventional or strange to others, but it is essential to explore and pursue them. We should be able to embrace our own quirks and interests and not be afraid to share them because that is us at our authentic selves, and we need to show that if we want to build genuine connections with others.

Currently, I have built up a considerable collection of critters that can entertain my children's friends. Whenever we have birthday parties or any gathering, I always show off my collection. However, my main objective is to introduce people to something new and unique and encourage them to appreciate it.

Last year, we moved to Alberta, and I had to figure out a way to feed my snakes without breaking the bank. Initially, I fed them chicken heads, but I couldn't find a steady supply here.

Fortunately, I discovered a Hutterite colony south of my

town that processes various birds. I called them up to order some chicken heads. When the man on the phone asked why I needed them, I explained that it was for my snake. With a rough, sort of German accent, he said, "A snake!? I've never seen a snake before."

He asked if I could bring it down to show him and his co-workers during their break. And of course, I agreed, and it was an enjoyable experience for all of us.

The art of exploring and embracing your quirks can lead to unexpected opportunities and experiences. My interest in reptiles allowed me to connect with members of the Hutterite colony.

I had the opportunity to introduce a new experience to others. Sometimes our interests can bring joy, not only to ourselves, but to those around us as well.

My enthusiasm for showing people something they may find new and interesting has been a great driving force in my life.

In my line of work, I take an immense amount of joy in enabling coaches and clients to uncover fresh insights about individuals that they may have previously overlooked or underestimated. I have come to understand the value of asking questions that delve deeper into an individual's character and experiences.

Often, we make assumptions based on surface-level observations or preconceived notions of someone, but it is only by digging deeper that we can truly uncover the intricacies of their personality.

I have found this to be highly effective in gaining a better understanding of teams and individuals. By taking a more nuanced approach, you can tailor leadership strategies to better meet the needs of the people you work with.

It's okay to be weird. Accept the strange and embrace the unfamiliar. That's how I went on my journey of discovery.

Why Turn Over the Rock?

My personal motto is "Turn over the rock carefully."

It has a sizable risk-taking component to it, because I believe there is always something worth discovering. But it also promotes exercising caution to manage risks that may discourage exploration.

No matter where you look, there is always something valuable to discover, and with some careful planning, you can mitigate the risks. There are many ways to do things in a safe way, such as using a stick, instead of your hand, to turn over a rock.

I have always had a fascination for Australia, and it is definitely one of my bucket list places to go because of its amazing diversity and wildlife. However, I noticed that many people hold a common assumption about the country that perpetuates a certain fear of the unknown, in that they believe that everything in Australia wants to kill you.

To me, this is such a narrow and limited perspective. The thing is, if we are ready to take a chance and welcome the strange, there is so much beauty to be found. This is a mindset that can be applied to all aspects of life. We shouldn't let fear of the unknown prevent us from attempting to find new and even weird things.

There are always strategies you can adopt to minimize risks and experience new things safely without giving up your excitement and exploration.

This book is a journey of discovery, and it will encourage you to stoke your curiosity so you can ask the right questions. To ask questions, one must first have an inquiring, curious mind, and that curiosity will be ignited by realizing that there are countless discoveries to be made in life.

The doorway to all learning and opportunity is curiosity. My goal is to give you a comprehensive and focused guide to inspire your curiosity and help you cultivate your desire to connect and engage with people in meaningful ways.

My intention is for this book to serve as a platform for me to share some of my journeys as well as the things I have learned about direct outreach, including how to approach people and how to look at them on an individual basis versus a collective basis.

We have turned into a society of networking that sends blast invites to people without taking the time to truly discover who they are. I believe this book can offer a complementary approach, one that emphasizes patient discovery and a genuine sense of wonder and curiosity. An approach that takes the time to peel back the layers to uncover an individual's distinct characteristics and oddities.

Rather than blasting out a message and hoping to catch someone's attention, I encourage a more deliberate and thoughtful approach to networking centered on building connections.

In this fast-paced world, we easily get caught up in daily routines, rushing from one task to the next, without pausing and taking the time to understand our deeper motivations and desires.

That's where this book comes in. It's a guide to discovering what lies beneath the surface, whether it's in our personal lives, business ventures, or unique passions.

This book is about exploring the hidden depths of what drives us, so we can gain a better understanding of ourselves and those around us.

This journey is about being open to suspending our beliefs and judgments of ourselves and others. It's a reminder to be open to the possibility that a person, a situation, or a thing, is simply more than what meets the eye.

This is not an easy thing to do, especially in a world that values quick judgments and snap decisions to get ahead of everyone else. But when we take the time to truly understand the people and the things that surround us, we can uncover golden nuggets that make life worth living.

For some, those nuggets may be found in the natural world. For others, it may be in the people they meet and the relationships they form. But regardless of where they are found, one thing is certain, they are worth seeking out.

That journey started for me when I got into consulting. I paid someone to show me how to do something, and it led to many great things I didn't realize were possible. I recognized the value of seeking guidance and expertise from others who could teach me what I didn't know.

I have come to appreciate the importance of staying curious, being open-minded, and embracing the journey that comes with this mindset. I believe that it is through this way of thinking that we can truly expand our under-standing of the world and our place within it.

The journey of discovery is ongoing, and I am committed to exploring it for as long as I can.

– Tyson Knauf, February 2024

Chapter 1

Wild Quail

W hen I reflect on my personal experiences, there is one from my childhood that stands out as particularly instructive–my encounter with a wild quail.

It was an experience that left me with invaluable insights into building trust in any human interaction, particularly in the business world.

Approaching someone for the first time is akin to encountering a flighty bird. If you come at them with only your own agenda, they will likely bolt at the first opportunity.

Just like in an initial interaction with a potential client or partner, there is a crucial moment of decision. Will they stick around or fly away?

It is for this reason that I find it fitting, even necessary, to begin my book with the story of this encounter, as it illustrates the importance of cultivating qualities like patience, observation, and collaboration, which can pave the way for establishing trust and finding solutions.

As a child, I spent many afternoons playing with bugs on the sidewalk next to Wade's house. Wade was my elderly neighbor, who I would often visit to help with his computer or other small tasks. He had known me since I was a kid because my grandma had lived in his basement suite.

One day, he came over to see if I could help with a quail that had found its way into his woodwork shed. With my dad in tow, we made our way to the shed.

While Wade and my dad stood outside, I edged in and saw the quail flapping against the east-facing window inside. Eventually, the quail grew tired and stopped moving.

I went in, and I approached the bird; it didn't seem to be alarmed, and it even turned toward me at that point.

Then I remembered that when we had kept budgies, if we wanted one of them to perch on our hand, we needed to put a finger underneath its breast so it could step up on it.

With that experience in mind, I thought I'd just do the same thing and see what happened. I waited until the quail was still, and then held my hand out to see if it was bothered, but it seemed fine.

Then, I put my index finger underneath its breast, and it hopped onto my finger, standing still. I was unsure what would happen next, so I slowly walked out with the quail on my finger. I thought it would fly away as soon as it saw the door, but it held on.

When I reached Dad and Wade outside, I threw the quail up, and that's when it flew away. Both of them were surprised by what they had witnessed.

Although I did not think much of it at the time, looking back, I realize that my love for nature and the joy I receive from connecting with animals made the interaction with the quail feel like a natural occurrence.

I knew that the bird had wanted a less restrictive option based on observation and my experience with the budgies we had kept. Back then, I noticed that if we tried to grab one to bring it out of its cage, it would get agitated.

However, when we offered our finger to one of them to perch on, it would remain calm. I had observed the budgies' behavior for a while and identified a pattern or thought process that is typical among birds. So as a kid, I had previously experimented with their likes and dislikes.

Before attempting to help the wild quail, I observed not only the bird but what the bird wanted, because it was indicating exactly what it wanted. It wanted to get out of that woodwork shed, but the only way out it could see wasn't working.

In situations like this, you need to sit back, observe what the bird is doing and then collaborate. I allowed it to struggle and come to its conclusions before presenting it with any options.

As soon as it had exhausted all of its options, it was more receptive to other ideas. But I knew that if I had intervened earlier, it would have freaked out and wouldn't have trusted me.

I believe that when you first meet someone, it's similar to encountering a flighty bird. They could just as easily fly away as stay and talk to you, especially when there's no foundation of trust between you, and they don't feel like they need to accommodate you.

If you approach with only your own agenda in mind, they will likely fly away. However, if you invest the time to listen, ask good questions, and seek to understand them, that's when the foundation of trust is laid.

I grew up in an urban neighborhood in West Kelowna, British Columbia, Canada. My house was at the end of the street, with only Wade's house next to it.

Known as 'Napa Valley North,' Kelowna is full of fruit orchards and vineyards, and I happened to live really near to an orchard, which is now a vineyard. Springtime in the orchard was breathtaking, with apple blossoms covering the trees and the melodic noises of California quail filling the air.

I remember the male California quails had a remarkable black color around their eyes and a big plume above their heads, which was their trademark feature. Their breasts were covered with brown and white speckled plumage, and they scurried all around the neighborhood in little bands.

Our house was located on the edge of a forest causeway, so we would often spot coyotes and deer wandering in the orchard. The area was abundant with wildlife, and during springtime, it was an absolute paradise with beautiful birds like magpies and finches chirping away. We even had great horned owls nesting around our house.

It was a neat area to grow up in. I always felt surrounded by nature, even though it was an urban neighborhood.

Because we lived so close by, Wade and I got to know each other quite well. His wife was still alive for much of my childhood, but unfortunately, she later passed away from cancer.

I was always going over to their place when my grandma used to live in their house. Leona, Wade's wife, would always make us cookies, a classic neighborly gesture that I enjoyed as a kid. Although they didn't have children of their own, Wade and Leona seemed to really enjoy having us around.

I'm the second youngest of five kids in my family, and I was probably the most consistent one in going over to Wade's house. When Wade got a computer in the early to mid-90s, he often called me over to help him use it. At 14, I was happy to oblige.

I remember that soon after Leona passed away, Wade was on his own, and I would help him out with various things. By trade, Wade was a sign maker and had a wood workshop that was separate from the house.

On the day that he left the door open and the quail flew in, his immediate thought was to call me over for help because he knew that I was interested in wildlife and loved playing with the bugs on the sidewalk.

Wade spoke to my dad, and my dad came to get me saying, "Hey, Wade's got a quail in his shop," and I remember getting pretty excited.

It's a common occurrence for people to think of me when it comes to anything to do with wildlife. My sister always sends me pictures of lizards, rattlesnakes, and bears from the rural area she lives in. Wade was similar in that regard, knowing that I would be eager to help with anything wildlife-related.

He had tried to get the quail out of his workshop by himself, but he was worried that he might hurt it without a proper net.

Going into the shed, I didn't have a specific plan for how to rescue the quail. I had an idea of what might happen, but I didn't come prepared with a net, nor did I intend to capture it. Instead, I allowed it to express whatever it needed to, whether it was frustration or exhaustion from flying against the window.

After it had expended its energy and was tired enough, I offered it a choice. I didn't impose a scenario on it; rather, I presented it with options.

I believe that with birds, allowing them to perch on your finger makes them feel safe, not threatened. If I had attempted to seize the bird, it would have been a different story. Instead, throughout the encounter, the bird felt in control and knew that it could take off at any moment and be fine.

In professional relationships, I take a similar approach. I don't enter with an agenda to force things and try to surround a person with what I want. Rather, I let them express themselves and take the time to understand them. Once they have expressed themselves, I offer them choices. And I kind of give up my options in a way.

Allowing them the freedom to set the agenda, set the stage, and being willing to be flexible enough to go with that creates one of the first building blocks of trust. If the quail hadn't hopped onto my finger, I would've sought out other options, such as birdseed. Fortunately, the first option worked out.

In any situation with a person, you cannot tell them what to do. All you can do is give them options and when you do, you allow them to make a choice. This approach works in business, personal relationships, and even in parenting.

When I talk to clients or potential clients, my approach is always aimed at helping them, even if that means referring them to someone else. I tell them, "I'm here to help, but you can hop off whenever you want because the main goal is to help you."

One of the fundamental keys to building trust with a bird is to ensure that it feels free and in control. Birds have an innate desire for freedom, and they never want to feel trapped and held down.

By allowing them the space to exercise their freedom, you can create an environment of trust and persuade them to do what is best while still respecting their need for autonomy. The same analogy applies to building trust and fostering healthy relationships with a person.

The bird probably didn't have it in its mind that it could climb up on my hand, but it did know that it liked to perch on things because then it could still fly away if it felt it needed to.

In the same way, when I offer people options, I leave them open-ended, allowing them to decide if it's a fit. If it doesn't work out, that's fine. The key is to ensure that they have full agency over their decisions.

Once I presented my finger to the bird, it was ultimately the bird's decision to come up onto my hand.

Timing is a critical component when offering options to people as well. There's no use in talking to them when they're still trying to get out of their situation on their own.

If they're still flying and flapping against the window, you have to just let them do that and acknowledge that the timing isn't right. It doesn't mean that you can't be there for them when they struggle. But once they're settled and say, "I can't do this on my own," that's when you'll want to be there for them.

It's not like that trapped quail understood my intentions, but it knew to stay upon my finger. My role was to be there and provide options for the bird, but it was up to it to choose its own path. Eventually, we reached our destination, and I let it go on its way.

I know I didn't get any referrals out of that one, but damn, that was a good experience.

The metaphor of standing on lily pads comes to mind when I think of situations like that. People may hesitate to put their full weight on someone else due to a lack of trust.

We must actively seek to understand others, their feelings, and their thoughts in challenging moments, because being present and merely occupying space is a passive approach and is not enough.

To understand is not to relate, because the latter is a self-centered approach that disregards the unique experiences of those being observed. With people, it's about allowing them to share their own thoughts and holding a space for them to be heard.

Give them options that are comfortable for them, too. It would have been uncomfortable for the quail had I gone after it and tried to grab it with my hands. That would have only scared it. So I gave it something to perch on, something to hang on to, allowing it to feel supported and pursue its goals.

I could have come in with a net or a box or something like that too, but that wouldn't have been liberating for the bird. That would actually have had the opposite effect. And it most likely would have left with a negative impression of me because of that interaction.

I believe that occasionally, we figure out solutions that are more complex than necessary. Just like going and getting a box or a net to rescue that quail would have been too complex.

Oftentimes it's simply about supporting others, which is a more nuanced approach that recognizes the complexities of each individual's situation.

In relationships, the power of support is often underestimated. It's like, "Whether I help you or not, I'm happy to be there to support you and be a positive source for you in whatever way you need."

Whether someone actually takes your support or not, that approach opens up the option of a partnership that could enable you to work together and move in one direction.

But before any of that, there is a trust hurdle that has to be overcome. And to establish that trust, you need to come with an open mind, a clear agenda, and an unwavering interest to attentively listen and comprehend. Only then will you know what options to offer.

In the realm of trust-building, it's like offering a bird a sturdy branch to perch on. If the branch is flimsy, the bird won't feel safe to stand on it. Similarly, trust takes time and is something to be built upon.

To establish trust, it's crucial to enter meetings with an open agenda, devoid of preconceived notions or fixed goals.

In any journey, there are steps to be taken. I call the following steps 'Tyson's Wild California Quail Trust Exercise!'

It involves patiently approaching a wild quail (or person) with the intention of gaining their trust and creating a connection based on mutual understanding.

And if you happen to be a wild quail, please don't peck my readers' eyes out!

Observe Them

The fear of vulnerability is an understandable one. It's natural to be afraid of putting yourself out there and potentially getting hurt in the process.

The fear of birds could be used as a metaphor for this fear of vulnerability. Because birds, like humans, can be unpredictable, and their behavior can be difficult to anticipate. Like, 'If I extend myself and if I put my heart out there, are they going to peck it out?'

As I was approaching the quail, I cautiously peered through the door to locate it, as I was unsure where it was. Soon enough, I spotted it by the window, and it was focused on the window, so I didn't feel as scared.

It was so engrossed in its concerns that I didn't think it would notice me. Once it settled, it turned towards me, and I waited until it was calm enough. Initially, I had concerns about the bird's sharp claws and beak, but I never really felt afraid of getting my eyes pecked.

But as it dawned on me that I could potentially get it to perch on my finger, my apprehension diminished, and I thought it would be really cool. Once I saw the possible solution, it didn't seem as scary. The key was taking the time to understand the situation better.

I had to overcome the fear of the unknown, too. Like the closed door that lay ahead of me before I was able to locate the bird, it was intimidating.

There are countless possibilities and uncertainties that can run through one's mind. Could this bird be a mother bird? Is it going to fly out underneath my feet? Anything moving around your feet can sometimes be scary, like mice running around the floor.

When I went in there, and it calmed down, my confidence grew a bit more. When I meet with people and I take a moment to be calm, it always boosts my confidence. It's in the state of calmness that the magic happens.

Your potential clients need to at least have tried something before seeking help. If they haven't tried anything yet, it means they haven't put in enough effort. They may have tried things on their own, or they may not have, but they need to be at a stage where they can realize that they can't do it alone.

They can come to that conclusion very early, or later on, and that's okay. But they need to get to that point where they acknowledge their inability to handle their situation on their own and become open to ideas.

So when it comes to it, a prospect isn't a prospect until they recognize the need for external assistance and support from someone with expertise.

As for the bird, perhaps my confidence gave it the impression that I knew what I was doing. At least, maybe it did!

Seek to Understand

The first thing to know when approaching a bird is how crucial it is to observe its reaction to your movements. A good sign is when you start moving your hand toward it, and it doesn't react.

To avoid being threatening, keep your hand low and offer your finger. Once you are close enough and the bird remains calm, you can gently place your finger in front of it, so it can step on it.

Seeking to understand is the key when it comes to interactions with birds or people. Pay attention to how people respond to your questions, to certain thoughts and ideas, and if they respond positively or negatively. Then you can adjust your approach.

For instance, if the bird had lowered itself and started to flap its wings, I would have stopped approaching and made myself appear less imposing by kneeling down. I had a pretty decent height for my age back then, I was probably at least five feet ten inches, which means I would've looked like a big predator to it.

The fact that the quail didn't freak out is actually kind of impressive when I think about it. However, I believe it was because it was at the end of its rope and was willing to try things it wouldn't normally attempt.

Fortunately, I think my approach helped me not appear as a predator. Instead, I came across as a support, much like a tree. Then I was something that it recognized as a perch instead of something to avoid getting eaten by.

Something to Perch On

Be a perch instead of a predator.

The concept of becoming a perch rather than a predator applies to interactions with business prospects as well. It's crucial to position yourself as a helpful resource instead of a threat.

By being a perch, you can help them see you as someone they can rely on for support instead of someone to avoid.

With a lot of clients, there seems to be an innate and natural tendency to view situations as threatening. If you can take the threat out of it, opportunities will arise, and creativity will flow.

It's difficult for creativity to flourish in a panicked mindset. That's why trust is essential as a foundation, because it unlocks creative potential. Without trust, the creative process is hindered.

Once we establish the problem and identify the gap between where the client is and where they want to be, my role is to simply show them the perch.

In my case, it's showing them what my process is to help them get to where they want to go. I help them to see that by allowing them to take control of the conversation and ask me questions.

This is when they are essentially testing the waters with their feet. Then they bring up their concerns, and I try to address each one of them.

Once they have explored all possible threats and think, 'Oh, this is something I can hang my hat on,' or 'I can stand my foot on this,' then they can make an informed decision on whether to proceed with me as a support.

As we reach this point, I hand over the conversation to the client. In most cases, I spend the initial part of a sales call asking questions to fully understand their situation. Once I understand the details clearly enough, I shift the conversation to explain what I do and how I can help.

I provide them with an overview of my services, but ultimately, the decision is theirs. They then go into the process of feeling out if there is support for them against any perceived threats.

This serves as the ultimate test, where objection handling and probing questions take place. For me, it's like being in the 'hot seat.'

Recently, I met with three potential partners, one at a time. The third partner put me firmly in the hot seat and came at me with questions like, "What's the worst thing people say about your clients? What's the best thing?"

It was a moment when it became clear that we still had a lot of building blocks of trust to work on. But this was a paramount part of the process to move forward, and I always welcome the challenge.

Whether or not it was a fit was out of my hands, but I wanted to make sure they knew what their options were and what the road ahead looked like.

Just like the bird that had the option to hop on my hand, you have to hand people the reins to do that. It's about providing a perch and allowing them to be able to put some weight on that perch.

In some ways, being an open book is also essential. You have to make them feel comfortable to put their weight on you and test you as a perch by asking relevant questions. On your part, you then can't conceal any relevant information you have.

Guide Them

Like with the wild quail, I let potential clients know that I'm there to support them, and I'm not there to eat them.

I try to keep the interaction ride as smooth as possible for them, so I keep a pretty steady hand.

It's important to keep things flowing, especially at the beginning, so I take it slow to start with while also letting people know the direction we're headed in.

With the quail, I knew that it could feel whether or not my finger was steady. And I guess that was the only way we were communicating at that point, through the steadiness of my hand.

As I was walking out of that shed, it felt supported enough to not want to fly away instantly. If I had dropped my hand at any point, it would have flown away or flown deeper into the workshop.

As soon as we were outside, I hoisted it up in the air. It could have stayed on my finger, because I wasn't committed to throwing it off, but it chose to fly away.

That's how I approach the client's life cycle. If a client outgrows me, it's a good thing. I'm happy to provide options and connect them with people who can help them grow beyond my capabilities.

It was like that with my first executive coaching client. He grew into group coaching, and that was outside my realm, so I connected him with people on Facebook that could do marketing campaigns for him.

We understood each other enough to know where he was going and that it was above and beyond me, so I was happy to give him the option of getting to where he wanted to go.

Let Them Fly Away

Sometimes we try to hold on to clients or relationships, but it's essential to provide enough value and allow them to become independent. Coaches may feel good when their clients need them, but it's important for them to let their clients fly and grow on their own.

As a coach, I'm here to support and guide them back if needed, but I don't want to clip their wings. Letting them fly and supporting their growth is the ultimate goal. We need to acknowledge if it's outside of, or beyond, our capabilities.

We don't have to be everything to everyone all the time, either. Do what you're good at, but then allow clients to outgrow you, too. I think that's totally cool.

I didn't expect the wild quail to come back to the shed with friends or to form a lasting bond with it. But in that one small positive interaction, I felt I could make a difference. I helped it feel that it was supported by something, a higher power, or by someone that was meek enough to help it.

It was really cool just to help one creature. It's important to me that when I am in a position of power where I can help or hinder someone, that I choose to help them. It's a principle that can be applied in business as well.

With power, you can hurt people, or you can make the right decision to help them instead. It's a good eternal law to follow.

There is no doubt that there are business people who come like a wolf in sheep's clothing. They say they want to help, but often, there is an underlying agenda there.

You have to approach each interaction without an agenda. It's about being willing to offer help but at the same time, respecting someone's decision if they say they don't want it.

Sometimes, people worry too much when people don't ask for their help, and they attach their worth to whether they can be of help or not to others.

You can still extend help from a distance by letting them finish exploring their options first and allowing them full agency to make a decision about what they need out of their situation. Trust goes both ways.

In business, it's easy to feel the pressure to help everyone and become frustrated if someone doesn't take our help.

However, we need to understand that it's not about us, it's about the people we're trying to help. They may not trust us yet, or they need more time to gather more information to make a decision.

With an agenda-free approach, we can create positive experiences and make a difference, no matter how small.

Every interaction, even if it doesn't go as planned, is an opportunity to learn and improve. There are truly no negative interactions because they all provide feedback that can help you better help someone the next time.

Eventually, you may reach a point where you can support others without feeling like you need to lean forward too much and take control.

When approaching clients, don't rush it. In any interaction where you aim to build a foundation of trust, you have to match their pace. Just like with the quail, I had to move slowly and give it options, without approaching it like a predator. It's the same when interacting with people. Observe them long enough and then match their pace.

And give them time to struggle, too. If they're not done struggling yet, then you need to let them struggle longer. But when they go still and are finally listening, that's when they are ready. Being able to recognize these two things is crucial.

I believe that confidence in this role stems from under-standing timing, too. Either the timing is right for me to be a support for them, or the timing isn't right for them to take my support.

Every client and prospect has their own readiness level. Not everyone is ready to take the next step, and that's okay.

It would be interesting to see if the last four or five clients I took on board were all at the same level of readiness, but that's not really possible.

Don't get caught up too much in the timing of it all, just be patient and understanding with each client's individual needs.

I think my calmness and ability to establish trust with animals in my childhood has helped develop and strengthen my calm demeanor of the present.

In my opinion, when one can gain the trust of a wild animal, building trust with people becomes easier. So, give people a solid foundation to plant their feet on and feel supported, because that's all they want.

I have no doubt that my prior experience in calming wild animals is now being applied to helping people feel at ease. In a sense, I have transitioned to taming people instead of animals.

Since I was willing to take the time back then, it's not much of a stretch for me to take that same time with my clients now.

In a world where trust is hard to come by, sometimes the key to building relationships is simply to become a perch rather than a predator.

Chapter 2

Snakes

I have found that people will often think of all snakes as being bad creatures. However, I think that people, in general, are also like snakes in that they have good, bad, and diverse personality types.

Every snake is different. I've got two snakes right now. One's an Australian Olive Python, and the other one is a Madagascar Dumeril's Boa.

In the wild, Madagascar Dumeril's Boas sit in the foliage and wait for something to come by before they grab it.

Australian Olive Pythons, on the other hand, are hunters. If they see a bird in a tree, they'll literally go up there and get it. They seem highly intelligent as far as snakes go, but they're also very obtuse in a way.

They're a bit of a paradox in that people call them gentle giants, but at the same time, they have a really high feeding response. You can never fully trust one to not bite you.

On the other hand, my Dumeril's Boa, I trust 99.9%. Kids handle him, and he's super chill, just like a puppy dog.

I used to have another Olive Python, six years ago, and I thought it was the coolest thing ever. But I didn't realize how unpredictable they could be. Mine had never properly bitten me, it tagged me once when I was feeding it, but it never wrapped me.

When they wrap you, they grab you and wrap around you, and don't let go. But that snake always used to let go of me right away.

He bit my dog once, but that's because the dog got up in his face. The python opened its mouth first to ward him off, but that didn't work, and my dog came back again, so it just tagged him.

I thought it seemed like he had his nuts in a row. But then, one day, something happened.

My son was holding the Olive Python, and at the time, he was only maybe about four. When I look back now, I realize it was the dumbest idea ever.

It was on my son's lap on the couch, and it was kind of just slithering around. Then it kind of went up to my son's nose and flicked it with his tongue, and I thought, 'Oh, that's cute.'

But then it just went bam! The python grabbed onto my son's nose and wrapped and hung on. So I had to go in and pry it off with my thumbs to get it away from him.

At the time, the snake was probably about six feet long, but only weighed a couple of kilos, so it wasn't too big. But after that, my wife said, "No, we can't have a snake anymore." So I sold it.

About four or five years later, when we moved out here, I got my own snake room, a separate room in the house with its own footings that was totally sealed off. That was what allowed me to get another Olive Python.

I really like the species because they seem highly intelligent in the way that they operate, and they're also very curious.

It's funny, because if you put my Dumeril's Boa on the couch, it'll try and climb into the couch, underneath the cushions, to hide. Whereas my Olive Python will actually go over things.

It doesn't really try to go into things, it goes over things, it's more of a climber. They're both very different.

Both my snakes also look really cool. Both species are probably some of the most painted and detailed animals there are. Their skin and their color patterns are very intentional, a lot more intentional than most animals. My Dumeril's Boa looks like dead leaves, because that's what they do, they hide in dead leaves.

My Olive Python has a lighter bottom. Its stomach is a whitish yellow, so you can't see it very well when it's above you in the trees. It's olive-brown on top, so if it's on the ground, it blends in with the ground better.

Snakes are probably the most intimate sort of pets you can have because their whole body wraps around you to get around. They're completely reliant on you when you're holding them.

My Dumeril's Boa, Max, is quite strong now. He weighs about eleven pounds.

If I have him on my neck, and he's trying to climb around, he'll hang on really tight. I have to give myself some room to breathe because he wants to be sure he's well-supported before he moves on to another spot.

I find that when you're holding a snake, it's a lot more of an intimate experience than holding a dog or something like that. A dog usually wants to get off you right away, whereas a snake is kind of reliant on you to some degree, in terms of being able to have you as an anchor to be able to move along.

As much as they are reliant on you, they're also very independent, as they don't really eat very often. Mine eat once every three weeks, so they're easy to take care of in that way.

If I go away for two weeks, I can fill their water dishes and those will last for about a week and a half, but then they're fine without water for a couple of days. They're quite hardy that way. They're cheap to feed, too. I feed them chicken heads and duck heads, and the occasional gopher or quail.

Thinking about what attracts me to snakes, I think it is mainly that intimate experience that comes with holding one. I don't think you can find that with any other animal. They look dangerous, but they're not necessarily dangerous.

People kind of have this sweeping view of snakes, when in reality, every species has its own temperament. You can build trust with snakes too, but I'd never trust them a hundred percent.

I got the Olive Python that I have now last December. He was maybe a couple of feet long and weighed about 500 grams at the time. He was small, but he would bite everything.

He was always biting my feeding hook. I put my hand in the cage just to see if he'd bite, and he totally bit it. But the bites aren't that bad. It's actually the fear of the bite that's worse.

It's funny because I'm still terrified of getting bitten, but when you get bitten, you think to yourself, 'Oh, that wasn't so bad.'

You think, 'Oh, you have nothing on me, it's no big deal.' I actually wanted him to bite me when I first got him, just so I could get used to him and fear him a lot less.

Over time, I tried to handle him once a day if I could, because you can sow threads of trust with snakes in terms of them getting used to the fact that you're not going to hurt them.

He's only been aggressive with me on one occasion, really. I had him outside, and I went to pick him up, and he kind of flared at me a bit. But generally speaking, he's pretty calm.

It's funny though, he'll be cruising along, and if he bumps into your hand, sometimes he'll stop and smell it. That's usually the sign for me that I should pull it away because he's going to try and bite me.

Having had him for over a year now, I find I'm able to tell when he shifts into that state. Snakes basically have four different kinds of states, or modes, that they can be in.

They've got their sleeping state when they're sleeping, they've got their defensive state when they want to defend themselves, and they've got their hunting state, when they're a predator looking to hunt. Then they have their curious state too.

That's the four modes that they can be in, and after a while of handling a snake, you can kind of pick up on their modes. And some snakes can change quite quickly, both for good and for bad.

Sometimes when I'm taking my python out of the cage, for instance, he'll be in predator mode. He'll be trying to hunt because he thinks, 'Okay, this might be a food opportunity.'

He behaves a bit differently in that mode. His eyes dilate, like something out of a movie. In that situation, all I'll do is open up the cage, and then I'll touch him on the tail, away from his head, to get him moving.

After doing that, he shifts states and acts like he wants to say, "Okay, what's going on?" I take him out then, and he's fine. He goes into his curious mode, where he's looking around, investigating, wanting to see what's going on.

That's the mode I want to have him in most of the time when I'm handling him. If I'm holding him, and he's wrapped around my neck or whatever, he'll constantly be investigating things around him.

'What's this? Let's smell it, let's taste it.' When I'm handling him in that mode, it's almost like looking after a toddler. I'm trying to just point him in the right direction. I'll give him some things to check out. I'll usually let him smell me a couple of times, too, so he gets used to my scent and taste.

I call him George, though he was originally named Declan. When I got him from a friend of mine, I didn't like his name, so I called him George.

He reminds me of Curious George because he's always looking into things. He likes to crawl over things and investigate things like, 'What's over there, what's in that little box?' He's always taking in his environment, and I find it really cool to watch.

When I hold Max, he takes in his environment too but tends to settle pretty quickly. George is forever cruising around and will only settle once he finds a spot that is warm enough.

When snakes are in curious mode, their eyes aren't dilated, they look more like slits, and they're just taking in their environment. They're asking, 'What's going on here?' When George is like that, I'll give him opportunities. I'll take him to the couch, or I'll take him outside if it's warm enough.

It's interesting, when I take George outside for others to see, people say, "You take him outside and put him on your lawn, doesn't he just take off?" The interesting thing is, probably because he's inside most of his life, when you take him outside, he tends to smell each individual blade of grass as he goes along. He just sits there, taking in his surroundings.

When I put him in the grass, it might take him a good 45 minutes to decide to leave it because he's busy cruising around. When they're in that curious mode, they're just taking in their environment, they're processing what's going on and whether it's safe or not.

There's a guy I follow online, he's called New England Reptiles, they call him NERD for short, and he's kind of a reptile whisperer. I got the idea of the different modes of snakes from him.

If you know what mode a snake is in, you can manage them really well. And after a while of handling them, you will intuitively think, 'Okay, yeah, he's kind of wondering if that's food or not.' Then you can shift gears.

So when you're handling a snake, and it looks quite calm, and it is calm, you still need to constantly be assessing what mode it's in.

'Is he curious? Is he aggressive? Is he hungry? Is he hunting me right now?'

George, for instance, loves that I have a desk with two monitors and a pole. He loves to crawl all over it, but if he's off of me, and I become a third party to him, then he often goes into hunting mode.

If I'm at my desk typing away, and he sees my fingers moving or my hand moving around grabbing the mouse, he thinks, 'Oh, that looks interesting.' Then he comes in nice and slow, and I think, 'Okay, if he gets any closer, he's going to bite me.'

So then I turn around and touch his tail. Once I touch his back end, he gets moving, then I see him shift gears. He thinks, 'Okay, I'm getting curious again,' and snaps out of his hunting state.

I find that I'm always managing the states that my snakes are in.

I have to do that more with George than I do with Max. Max is usually in curious mode or sleep mode. Those are his two. If he smells a chicken, then he'll grab a chicken or whatever, but he differentiates between things that are food and things that aren't food, quite well.

With George, I'm always managing the mode that he's in because it can shift very quickly. He's very diverse that way.

I've got one client right now who's very diverse in the different modes that they can be in. Sometimes they'll say, "I want this, and I want that." We often call those people dramatic, but really, they're just very diverse in their mindsets.

I think that looking at it that way helps me to realize that it's not a matter of them being good or bad people but rather, 'They're in a mode, and how do I manage that? How do I approach that?'

If they're in a mode where they're feeling defensive, or they're feeling fearful, you can identify it and address it.

People have a lot more modes than snakes do, but once you understand what mode someone's in, then you can ask yourself, 'Okay, how do I address that? How do I respond to that and manage that state that they're in?'

I guess the answer comes with practice. I don't know if I'm there with people as much as I am with snakes, but I've found that being calm no matter what always helps.

When dealing with some people, maybe under the surface, you're thinking, 'Okay, how are they going to respond to this, how are they going to respond to that?' But once you understand their different mindsets, that takes away the mystery and the fear.

If you understand, 'Oh, this person's fearful because of this,' you can then work to address that.

Whereas, If we say that someone is just being dramatic, then we actually don't understand the state that they're in, and we're just in defense mode. We're trying to defend ourselves from the unknown.

But once you understand the state that they're in, then it's not dramatic. It's just realizing, 'They're feeling fearful because of this,' or 'They're feeling frustrated because of this.' Then you can address the problem together. It's no longer a mystery.

The first client I ever worked with was a guy called Don Osmond Jr. He comes from the Osmond family, who were a big singing family in the 1970s.

Donny Osmond, who's the father of the family, is the main singer, and his son, Don Jr. was actually friends with my sister.

They got to know each other through church youth camps in the summer. Because of this, my family and I actually got to meet Donny Sr. when we headed down to a show he did with his wife Marie in Las Vegas in the early 2000s.

When I first started doing LinkedIn outreach back in 2015, Don Jr. reached out to me and sent me an email. I noticed he had scraped my information, because I was connected with him on LinkedIn, and then sent the email out.

I responded back, "Hey Don, I noticed that you're doing a kind of mass email, how's that working for you? Is it working well?"

He replied, "It's kind of touch and go. Some of it's working, but not as well as I thought."

I explained what I was doing in terms of direct outreach on LinkedIn itself. We set up a call, and on the call, I was asking him, "What's preventing you from doing better? Actually marketing yourself and connecting with clients?"

He was starting to get a bit mad, but luckily I stuck it out without getting too fearful. He said, "You keep asking this, why do you keep asking that?"

His company was a marketing branding company. He would take a company, understand their story, and then explain their story in a marketing context. He had spoken about it once at South by Southwest, down in Austin, Texas, with his dad.

He had quite a lot of influence, so I remember thinking, 'Why is he coming to me? Why is he interested in what I do?'

So I said to him, "You know, you've got this marketing company, but you're struggling to find clients, so tell me more about that, what's going on?"

That's when he loosened up, he said, "Well, you know, the thing is, I've been able to get clients through my family connections, and that has worked really well, but I've never found a client completely on my own."

He was wanting to get out from under the shadow of his family name.

After that, I realized that when people get angry on my discovery calls, or when they get upset or frustrated, they're not angry at you, they're more angry at the circumstances that they're in, and that anger is a good thing.

It's usually a breakthrough in a lot of ways for them. I've had that myself too.

I had a business conversation with my wife a few months back, and I was getting frustrated, saying, "I don't know if I can charge more, I don't know what I'm worth."

Her observation was, "Well, you've had these clients that have been paying you for three years."

I was kind of frustrated with that, but then I thought, 'Yeah, you're right.' That ended up being a big breakthrough for me in terms of knowing my value and sticking with it.

On the calls I do, I try to understand if a client is feeling frustration or pain, or anger.

If there is, for example, frustration, I'll try to figure out what the real cause of it is.

Once we understand what it is, then we can either come up with solutions that I can provide, or come up with solutions that I can refer to. Until we face the music and determine where things are really at and why, we really can't come up with the right solution.

With Don Jr., once we addressed his frustration and its cause, he was all on board. I explained what I do, and he said, "Yeah, that's totally what I need. I need someone that's taking my existing network and connecting me with them. Then I can build clients on my own instead of relying on my family's influence."

Coming back to my snakes, you can tell when they're feeling fearful or frustrated.

When they're fearful, they coil up, they get protective, and then they start moving inside their coil. If a snake is coiled, and it's moving inside its coil, that's not a good sign. It means it's not feeling comfortable in the state that it's in.

Once a snake starts to coil and move inside that coil, it'll start flicking its tongue and try to figure out what's going on in their environment as quickly as possible.

If one of my snakes does this, I instantly know I need to either sit back and let it feel comfortable again, or I need to kind of give it a prod to get it moving.

Once you get them to break their coil and move outside it, then they actually go back into their curious state again. It seems counter-intuitive, because normally, you don't poke a lion, but with a snake, it's fine once you actually get it to move again.

A few years back, in 2007, I was working down in Southern Okanagan. It's located in the far Northern part of the Sonoran Desert, where there's a lot of sagebrush.

I was out one night for a hike, and I stumbled across a rattlesnake. I heard it rattle first, and then I immediately jumped back.

In those situations, you think that, just like in the movies, you're going to stay calm and not move, but I jumped back before I even realized it. The snake was right in front of me, but he didn't strike at me.

He coiled up for a bit, but then he started to move and just rattled his tail as he moved away.

I actually went and picked him up. Rattlesnakes can't coil back on themselves, so if you pick them up by the tail, they're actually quite calm. It was the first time I had picked up a rattlesnake, but I had handled a lot of snakes at that point, so I wasn't feeling in deep water with it.

It's weird looking back. I didn't have my camera with me, so I put him in my backpack, zipped him up, and carried him along back to my car. My house was in Osoyoos, so it was maybe a five-minute drive to my house. I got my camera out, went back out to the desert, took him out, got a picture with him, and then put him down.

It was pretty cool because I'd never actually seen a rattlesnake in person before that.

If he had stayed coiled, I probably would have just left him alone. But because he started moving, I decided, 'Oh, he's not actually out to get me. He's actually pretty calm.' As it turns out, the Northern Pacific Rattlesnake is probably one of the most docile types of Rattlesnake.

Changing a snake's mode can look like snake charming from the outside, but really it's about managing their state and responding to it.

A lot of people will see a snake in one state and not understand that it's actually in another. They'll look at it coiled and think, 'It's trying to hunt me and attack me,' when really it's just afraid, and it's trying to defend itself.

If you can get the snake out of that fearful mode and get it moving, it will shift gears to a state like, 'Oh, what's in the ground here? What's over here?'

All of a sudden, it changes from a fearful mode to a

curious mode. And people don't realize that snakes can change modes very quickly like that, both in your favor and not in your favor.

We have Bull Snakes out around here in Kelowna, where I live, and they look a lot like rattlesnakes. They'll even separate their jaws to make their head look bigger like rattlesnakes do, and they'll hiss, and they'll flick their tails, but they don't have any rattle.

I was driving along once, and I ran one over, so I immediately pulled in. I thought, 'Oh man, I've killed it,' but he was still there, fine. He was coiled on the ground, and he didn't look injured at all.

I quickly realized, 'Oh, he is really mad.' I mean, obviously, he was; I had just run him over.

I don't remember if I grabbed a stick, or I just grabbed his tail, but I got him moving. Once he started to move, he was totally fine. I actually picked him up and put him in my bag. I brought him to the park because I decided to check him out and see if he was okay.

I took him out, and I was able to handle him just like a domestic snake because I had gotten him back into his curious state, where he was easy to work with.

I've been taking a course called Positive Intelligence, and the whole idea behind it is about changing your state of mind from a fearful state into a curious state. If you're fearful, you're kind of locked in that state, and the course suggests some exercises you can do to get out of that mindset.

They recommend you wiggle your toes or feel the pressure points in your feet as you're walking along. If you're sitting and stewing about a challenging situation, those exercises take you out of that state and put you into a curious state. In that curious state is where the magic happens in terms of getting ourselves out of difficult situations.

With clients, I try to break their fearful or angry or frustrated states. It's important to acknowledge it too, because that's what's going to give us a direction to move in.

Usually, in my sales calls, I tend to build up the pressure, essentially asking clients, "What's your state?"

I usually hear, "It's not where I want it to be, I don't know how to get out of it, I can't do it on my own."

Once they start saying those things, then I say, "Okay, let me explain a bit more about what I do, and if it's in line with what you're wanting, then I can walk you through what working together looks like."

"And if it's not, I'm connected with a lot of other people that might be able to help."

That takes them from their mode of frustration or anger to thinking, 'Oh, what does he do? Tell me more.' It gets them into a curious mode, and once they're in a curious mode, they're able to activate the innovative part of their mind.

Then, I can tell them what I do, and they can ask, "Okay, how would that fit with what I'm doing?" So then we're starting to go from a problem to figuring out how we can create solutions. Getting people into that state of curiosity is what breaks their defensive mode.

Acknowledgment is the first thing you need to work towards to get someone to respond to their state. And then you have to probe a bit.

You have to 'poke the snake.' People always say don't poke things, and I think there are things you definitely shouldn't poke, like some types of fuzzy caterpillars. But with snakes, you have to poke them a little bit to get them moving.

It's the same with people. While they do need to experience frustration or another negative state to understand what's bugging them, once they understand what that problem is, you must get them moving out of it.

You have to get them into a curious mode. It's like, "Now that we understand the problem that you have, can we talk about solutions here? Or can we talk about what I do?"

With a snake, when they're moving, they're looking for new opportunities, new environments, and new stimuli. So once you get them moving, you will want to provide them with stimuli to keep them going.

You can apply the same logic to how you work with clients.

Once you've talked about what their problem is, and you've defined it, they'll become curious, they'll start to move.

So once you get them moving, then it's about providing them with stimuli, like providing them with solutions or ideas that they haven't thought about before.

Once that part of their mind starts getting tripped, they

can think, 'Okay, how can this work for me?' At that point, it becomes a collaborative effort.

It's kind of the same with a snake. If you carry it on your shoulders, it becomes a collaborative effort rather than a single effort. Once you start to collaborate with a person, you can start to work together to come up with solutions, and no one is alone in that state.

Once someone sees their problem in fine detail, they can think, 'Okay, I can feel where I am, and I'll do whatever I can to get out of this situation.'

That, alone, piques their curiosity, so that they're actually listening.

Then I can ask, "Can I tell you more about what I do?" Then it's about explaining what they need to do in terms of the problem that they're faced with.

If they say, "I'm struggling to get clients; I don't know how to get clients on my own." Then what I do is I actually focus on finding their ideal clients.

Let's say, for example, that their ideal client is an executive who has reached a plateau in their career and doesn't know how to get to the next mountain.

I'll go and find CEOs that are in that state. I find them for my client and bring them into their network and start to engage with them on their behalf.

I poke them and prod them and see what state they're in. If they're in a state where they are frustrated or angry, then I pique their curiosity enough for them to want to learn more about my client's work.

We basically do the same thing that I do for my clients initially, in terms of defining their state, saying, "Okay, let's define the problem." I poke them enough to be able to find out what their real problem is, then we get clear on that.

Next, my client and I will set up an opportunity to engage with them, either on the phone or via Zoom. Then they might respond to my client when they realize, 'Okay, he's totally got the solution that matches my exact problem.'

Acknowledging Your State

When my dog went up to my python, it was not having it. I have often thought, 'Could that dog have ever convinced it to let him hold it?' I think the answer is no, probably not.

I think maybe it's built into the genes of snakes or something, but they can recognize a predator right away.

They don't really see me as a predator when I approach them. Maybe it's because I go in with a different approach, because often predators go right for the face. I think when someone or something goes for their face, snakes feel like they're being hunted or that they need to defend themselves.

If you come across a snake, and they're coiled, then you must stop. You need to look at them and figure out where they're at. Usually, at that point, I'll go and get a stick, not to hit them with, but rather to be able to prod them and to get them moving.

Sometimes in business, you can feel inadequate or caged or trapped, and if you feel that way, then often you might be looking for any way out of it.

That's the ideal sort of scenario, where you say, 'Yeah, I'm effed if I don't get out of this.'

It's all about acknowledging the state that you're in.

When I'm starting to work with a client, they may be at a stage where they feel pretty good, but then as we start to peel back the layers and I start to look at things, I might say to them, "Okay, if you continue along this path, where does it lead?"

That usually starts to get them into a state of realizing, 'Okay, maybe if I keep doing this, then what's at the end of this road is probably not positive.'

I need to open up their situation a bit more, but when I approach them at first, I need to put them in a relaxed state.

It's like that with a snake, too. I want to get them as relaxed as I can, as quickly as I can. If you get them moving, that gets them into that relaxed state.

With a person, you must engage them with small talk. You will want to connect and talk about things that are easy to talk about to start with. I always make sure to ask, "Tell me what got you into this business? What gets you excited?"

You want to get them from fearful to calm so that they're open to ideas and open to thoughts, but also open to sharing more about their situation. People are usually defensive at first, so you need to get them calm and curious.

At that point, then, it's all about exploring, and you'll just want to explore where things are.

Probe Yourself

If you find a coiled up snake, you must go to the back of it. You don't want to focus on the front of the snake. You can pick it up by the tail if you can get close, but if you can't, use a stick.

You can put a stick between their head and their tail, so you can grab their tail and get them moving without them striking or biting you. Once you grab their tail, you need to lift it a little bit, and then they'll start to move.

Then their immediate response will be like, 'Okay, let's move away from that, let's get moving.' I guess they get fearful. They go from being aggressive like, 'I can handle this myself,' to, 'Oh, yeah, I need to get away from this state.'

If you want to get moving, you need to consider where you are and where you want to be.

You need to think, 'What's my current state in fine detail? Where do I want to be, in fine detail?'

Once you understand those two states, you will know immediately if you can get where you want to be on your own, because you are automatically going to start assessing if you can do that yourself.

If you can, then great. If you can't, then okay, how do you bridge that gap? You must consider your options. By doing that, you're being open, and you can go into the state of being curious and wanting to find a solution.

The main thing is that you need to understand where you are and where you want to go and what that looks like in dollars, or in numbers, or in states of mind, or places you want to go and travel to.

Once you understand those two things, then, automatically, you're going to start assessing if you can get there and if you can do that on your own. It's either, 'Yes, I can,' or 'No, I can't.'

If you can't, then you must get curious. If you can, then great, awesome, you're good to go.

Move Forward

You might think a snake would just turn around and bite you once you get it moving. But when it's moving forward, I guess it must realize that it can't move backward.

So when you lift its tail, if it's not a tree snake, all it can do is try to get away from the situation. It will start to move in a direction that it feels is going to lead it to more safety.

In essence, you have to burn the ships for it. It's the only way it will move forward.

And it comes from them defining the state that they're in. Once they understand that they are in a challenging situation, they'll realize that they can either get pulled into some predator's mouth, or they can move forward.

It's funny, though, because they think very differently to humans in a way. When they start looking forward, they forget about everything else, and they think, 'Oh yeah, what's up here?'

Snakes are made to move forward. They like to move over things and feel the ground moving into their stomachs. Once they feel that, then all of a sudden, it's like their fear goes away somehow.

In order to move forward in business, you have to give up the fear. You can't hold onto it. You have to give it up and replace it with something new. You have to replace it with something that gets you excited or interested, or even just curious.

You have to feel like you're moving forward, and you have to start moving forward in a direction, and that can mean any direction in some cases. You've acknowledged where you're at, and now you need to start moving forward, whether it's by yourself or with other people who can help you.

It's an approach that's helped me throughout my business and my life.

Find New Stimuli

Once I get a snake moving, I'll actually pick them up. If it's a Rattlesnake, I'll pick it up by the tail and keep it picked up. But if it's a nonvenomous snake like a Bull Snake, then I'll pick it up, and I'll start doing this motion that stimulates them and makes them feel like they're moving forward.

Once you pick them up, then all of a sudden, they change. They switch states to, 'Oh, what's going on?' They don't know what's going on, but it's not unfamiliar enough that they feel like they have no idea what's going on.

They'll think, 'Okay, this is different, but I'm cruising, I'm moving. I'm getting the locomotion I want in order to feel like I'm moving forward.'

They go into that curious mode, and they kind of stay there. Unless you touch them on the face, then they'll retract a bit, and you have to get them moving forward again, or they're going to get defensive. You have to leave their vision and their senses wide open, while also stimulating them to move forward.

An example of new stimuli in business is a revenue target. You might be in a position where you're making X amount right now with your business. You might want to have an additional six clients a month and keep those clients for three months. On the numbers side of it, if you charge 10 grand per client, then that's 60 grand in extra revenue.

It doesn't matter if you want to go from making 60 grand a year to making 120 grand a year, or 120 to making half a million a year. It's all about figuring out what the specific dollar target is. With that in mind, it's about thinking what would be different for you if you reached your target.

'Okay, what would it look like for my family? What would it look like for my business? Would I hire more staff? Would I be in charge of more people? Would I still be going solo and have more independence? Would that allow me to travel more?'

Some coaches I work with tend to like to travel. If you've got a consistent goal of what you intend to make every month, then you can start making plans.

It's about getting very specific about your revenue target and thinking about what it's going to look like in terms of your desires and dreams.

In my business, I really help people to paint out a clear picture of not only what their money goal is, but what that money will do.

Once clients have a clear vision of what that money will do, then we'll start moving forward together, and they'll say, "Okay, yeah, this is what I would do, this is what I want to accomplish."

Pique Your Curiosity

I think piquing your curiosity is all about allowing yourself the ability to paint that picture of what it would look like if you did achieve a certain goal.

You can do this by asking yourself questions like, 'Could I do 'x' on my own? What have I tried so far? What's worked? What hasn't worked?'

'Am I the type of person to figure things out? Am I the type of person who gets someone to figure things out for me? What's my personality type?'

Once you clear all that up, then you can decide, "Yeah, I can do this myself."

On the other hand, you might think, 'No, I can't do this on my own. I've tried everything. I'm not a good salesperson,' or 'I just want to focus on coaching clients, I don't really want to focus on getting clients. That's not my expertise.' Then that's when you might consider collaborating with someone like me to help you get where you want to go.

My approach to helping clients varies. It all depends on where their starting point is.

Some coaches don't even know who their clients are. The first step is about being able to define who that client is. "Who's your ideal client? What's your starting point? How far and wide do you want to cast the net? Do we need to cast the net to start with?"

Once we've determined that, then I go out and cast the net for them. It's then about drawing people in, getting them into that state where they're curious enough to want to hop on a call. Once you get to that stage, then I'll say, 'Okay, well, how good is my client at closing these people?'

My goal is to get my clients four, five, or six calls with potential customers. Once they've had those calls, we'll circle back and have a conversation about how they went. If they had five calls, and they didn't close anyone, then we dissect that a bit more in terms of what they're doing.

I get them to record their calls, and we'll go through it, and I'll coach them through the sales process. I might say, "Okay, you didn't get them moving, you just went right for their face. You didn't pique their curiosity enough, they just stayed in that skeptical, defensive mode the whole time."

If they're good at closing, then great, then I'll just provide them with opportunities. If they're not good at it, then I'll get them into that state where they are closing.

Sometimes I'll help prepare potential customers a bit for my clients before they hop on a call together. That way, they're already leaning towards collaborating, and my client just has to push them over. It's a bit of a joint effort that way.

I'll also work on my client's sales skills so that they can eventually turn a person that's skeptical into a client.

Being in the defensive state is kind of like holding your hand on a burner. When you put your hand on the burner, and you pull away, you change your state.

When we stay in a defensive state, it's like we're holding our hand on the burner when we really need to take it off and look at solutions. If we don't change that state, we become more and more coiled and more stuck in our ways. If we don't move, we're stuck, and we'll stay stuck until we decide to move.

The quicker you can move out of your defensive state, the quicker you can realize better states of mind to be in. Until you start moving, you're stuck, and you're not in a state where you can help yourself or others.

When people think of snakes, they always think of them as being defensive or aggressive. But when I think of snakes, I look at them as creatures that can be really curious and interested.

My goal with snakes is to get them into their curious and interested mode as quickly as possible so that I can see them in comfort. That way, I can see them behave much more naturally in their environment.

I do the same thing with people if they're in that same defensive state that I find snakes can get into.

When people visit me, even if they're fearful of my snakes, I've found that if I can get them into that curious mode right along with one of my snakes, then they'll both start to connect.

A lot of women, and some men, think, 'Oh, this snake is so gross.' But I say, "You should just try feeling it, because it feels like an expensive pair of boots."

That kind of shifts them from fearful to, 'Oh, do they actually?' I'm not only turning snakes into curious snakes. I'm turning people into curious people as well. If you can turn both of them at the same time, then you're creating an opportunity for them to learn something and experience something new.

Become curious and focus on getting other people curious as well. Get them out of their defensive mode. The only way to get them out of that mode is to stimulate them to move forward, either with ideas or engagement.

Until we move forward, we're always going to be stuck. Start moving forward and getting others moving forward as well. If you stay coiled, you can't experience anything new.

You're going to starve yourself. A snake can't feed itself when it's coiled. It can only feed itself when it's curious and exploring. You're losing ground the longer you stay coiled.

Chapter 3

Spiders

G race is an essential ingredient to getting off to a positive start in any relationship. It's also essential for ensuring the continuous development of a relationship.

The cultivation of successful relationships is a nuanced art, and it is grace that is essential to fostering lasting human connections, both personally and professionally.

In our relationship, my wife and I always extend the benefit of the doubt to each other, which helps eliminate the unknowns that can often drain our energy.

As a business coach, I've found that assuming my clients are always doing their best and approaching them with empathy and a growth mindset can lead to collaboration that identifies the root causes of their challenges and develops effective solutions.

The power of this approach is that it can result in stronger and more meaningful relationships with clients.

As humans, grace helps us to overcome fears, both legitimate and imagined. A similar quality can also be observed in animals through meekness, and I believe that it is something we can learn from.

For instance, my pet snake Max, who weighs around eleven pounds, could bite me at any moment, but he never does.

Recently, my sister-in-law brought over some dead chicks from her hatchery, and my niece and nephew wanted to watch Max eat them. They've held Max lots of times because he's such a calm, placid snake.

But to show them what he was capable of, I took the feeding tongs and just waved them in front of his head. He flicked his tongue twice and then bit it. I told my niece that Max could bite anyone anytime, but he chooses not to.

You see, being meek is not a weakness, but rather a display of inner strength. It is the ability to hold power over others without using it unnecessarily.

Meekness allows us to refrain from hurting others even when we have the power to do so, while grace creates a space for vulnerability and forgiveness.

When we combine these two qualities, we cultivate an environment of trust and understanding that can sustain even the most challenging relationships.

Without meekness, we risk dominating others, and without grace, we risk missing out on opportunities for growth and learning. Ultimately, building strong relationships requires us to embrace both meekness and grace in equal measure.

I believe that assuming that your clients are doing their best is a critical mindset to adopt in business.

For instance, when I started working with one of my clients, they had not closed any deals despite having had 18 sales calls in the previous month and a half.

Initially, my reaction was to question her approach. However, I reframed my mindset and approached the situation with curiosity. We then delved into the details and examined the gaps in her strategy.

Instead of taking an authoritative approach, I collaborated with her to identify solutions. Through this approach, we were able to find the root cause of her issue and develop a plan to address it.

It's important not to assume that your clients are not taking their leads and opportunities seriously. In fact, I have found that 99% of the time, clients are already doing that.

So, empathy is crucial. As a professional, it's my job to help my clients, but I cannot help them if I approach their situation with a negative attitude.

Giving people the benefit of the doubt is key to building strong relationships, whether it's with your clients or your employees. For example, when working with the virtual assistants I employ, I provide guidance and ideas but also give them the freedom to make decisions and work independently.

Interestingly, there is a certain meekness to spiders, and it's one of the most significant differences I've noticed between them and many of my other pets.

I currently own six tarantula spiders, and over the years, I've learned that they can be moody.

You can control the moods of snakes to some extent by handling them in a certain way. With many tarantulas, it's not possible to do that. You either have a docile breed, or you don't.

In your first interaction with them, tarantulas will always let you know whether they're open to being held or not. It's similar to the Hippogriff scene in Harry Potter, where if you bow to the creature, it will bow back if it likes you.

If you touch tarantulas on the rump while they are facing away from you, and they turn around, it means they don't want to be held or aren't convinced yet. And if you touch them again, they may try to bite you or raise their legs to warn you.

One of my tarantulas is a large Salmon Pink Birdeater Tarantula.

They are an interesting species because, especially when they are young, they tend to be aggressive, flighty, and defensive. But I can usually get mine out of that mood by using tongs to gently corral her around the cage.

Once she starts moving away from my hand, instead of turning to face it, I know she's okay. Then, I can reach in and scoop her up into my hand, and she'll be perfectly fine.

Years ago, when I got my first tarantula, I held it in my hand and noticed that it started to lose its grip when I turned my hand vertically. To my surprise, the tarantula used its fangs to hang on to the end of my finger, which was a harrowing experience at first. However, I quickly realized that it was actually quite gentle, as it was just using its fangs as a 10th pair of legs to get over the edge of my hand. Once it got up there, it was fine.

Although I've only had that experience once, I tend not to let my tarantulas crawl over the edge of my hand anymore because they could bite me at any time, especially once they're out of their cage.

Usually, tarantulas aren't like snakes that can surprise you with a bite; once you get a tarantula out of its domain and start to handle it, it becomes submissive.

However, it's important to remember that tarantulas could still bite you at any time, regardless of the environment. Although their venom is not usually harmful to humans, their two-inch fangs can still cause significant pain and discomfort.

A while back, I bought two Brazilian Black Tarantulas as babies. I was hoping to breed them because they sell for 60 bucks each as spider lings. They usually lay about 500 eggs, so I thought it would be cool, but they both turned out to be males.

Despite their reputation for being a calm species, one of these male tarantulas is the most flighty and aggressive spider I've ever owned. If I go near it, it starts flicking urticating hairs, which are fiberglass shards of hair with venom inside them that can cause hives and rashes if they get on your skin.

The other male is almost the same age, but is super calm and easy to handle. This shows that tarantulas have their own personalities, and they can be unpredictable.

My experience with these two spiders has taught me to respect boundaries.

The grace that comes with age has allowed me to appreciate my tarantulas more, particularly my Salmon Pink Birdeater. When I first acquired her, she was quite aggressive and would flick her hair at anything that came near her.

However, as she grew larger, she became more placid, as is often the case in the animal kingdom. With her size, she no longer needed to be so defensive. She's now a total wimp of a spider, despite being over six inches in size.

During the winter, I feed her my honeybees. If bees leave their hives in the winter, they'll die if they get too cold. If you pick them up and get them within a few hours, you can actually bring them inside, warm them up, and they come back to life again.

But my Birdeater will only eat them if they're not buzzing. If the bees are awake and start buzzing, she freaks out, and she won't eat them. So, I have to feed her one by one to get her used to the idea.

I put one in her enclosure, and if it doesn't buzz, she'll wait until it starts moving around before grabbing it and eating it. And by spoon-feeding her in that way, I've grown to appreciate her more.

I think the more effort you put in with pets, the more connected you become with them and the more appreciative you become of them.

I especially enjoy observing how my animals change as they grow.

My wife asked me one time, "Why do you do all of the things you do?" I always reply that it's because I like seeing things grow, develop and change.

I have Giant African Land Snails, which are actually illegal in Canada. I keep them in my compost bins along with Red Wiggler compost worms and springtails.

Together, they have a symbiotic relationship where the snails eat and mash up hard food and excrete it, and then the worms eat the snail's waste. The springtails, in turn, eat any molds and therefore prevent any from growing inside the bins.

I like observing the growth of the snails in particular, which I can see from the growth rings on their shells. I put a hot spring rock called 'tufa rock' in the compost bins, and they crunch it up and turn it into their shells.

I believe my fascination with growth and development is actually the common thread that ties together all of my pursuits.

In my experience, putting in effort and giving clients grace can promote growth, especially when working with coaches who are just starting out or getting back into coaching.

In contemplating grace, one may find that it hinges upon the recognition of growth that unfolds and takes place on a lot of different levels.

I have found that a deficit of grace arises from a desire to see growth in a single, specific area, especially when it proves elusive. But, if we broaden our perspective to acknowledge growth in all its forms, we are better poised to extend grace.

I recently collaborated with a coaching consultant based in Japan. He is a master coach with ICF, and he trains other coaches. I noticed that, despite his expertise, he was self-conscious on camera. So, I went about helping him to get more comfortable.

As I was walking him through the process during a session, I noticed that his intonation was really good. It's natural and posed, without any hint of artificiality. This is in stark contrast to many individuals, who struggle to maintain their authenticity when recording videos.

In recognizing his ability, I sought to encourage his progress, knowing that he tended to be hard on himself when it came to on-camera work.

I find it rewarding to help my clients recognize their strengths and witness their growth along the way.

Another of my clients, Nora, has been working with me for three years. During that time, we've discovered that her ideal clients are of Middle Eastern descent, live on the East Coast, and work in IT.

Nora is direct in her approach, which these clients appreciate, and they seem to have a natural affinity for her. Interestingly, Nora was born in France and spent most of her life there before moving to Seattle a decade or so ago.

We never would have guessed that her ideal clients would be from such a specific group. But over time, we've come to understand this dynamic and appreciate the beauty of how things unfold.

As a collector of tarantulas, I always want to have big, healthy ones. Feeding them and seeing their bellies grow bigger is really cool to me. Like with my other animals, I really enjoy watching their physical growth.

It's amazing to see them transform from looking like the tiny spiders that you would squash in the bathroom to gerbil-sized animals. I take photos every time they molt and put them into a shadow box on my shop's wall. Their molts look like tarantulas, and you can see how they've grown bigger and bigger over time.

Tarantulas show growth quite immediately. They may stay the same size for months, and then all of a sudden, they will molt and grow an inch and a half larger in diameter. Seeing their growth in such a quick time is gratifying, and it's unlike human growth, which usually occurs in increments.

My Salmon Pink Birdeater did not molt for almost a year. As she got closer to molting, the pink flesh on her abdomen darkened. Once it turned black, I knew she was soon going to molt. It was like an event, and I even did a time-lapse of her molting.

During molting, tarantulas lay down in a hammock made of web, flip upside down and just sit there for hours before their old skin slides off. Then, they stretch and move their fangs, which are still white because they haven't hardened yet.

In the world of coaching, I like to think there's a phenomenon that can also be described as the 'molting' of clients. Much like a tarantula sheds its old skin, clients undergo a transformation that is gradual yet dramatic. Their transformation is usually reflected in increased confidence, an ability to charge more money, and success in closing more deals.

For instance, a former British client named Jim had expressed a desire to charge more for his coaching services when we began working together. When I asked what was holding him back, he realized that the only thing standing in his way was himself. With newfound confidence, Jim gradually increased his rates from £3,000 to £4,000 and then to £5,000.

The results of us working together were immediate and tangible–he closed more deals and saw an increase in revenue. He started out doing one-on-one coaching and gradually expanded his business to include live events, public speaking events, and group coaching events. It was rewarding to see him eventually outgrow my services.

But the true measure of success for a coach is not in immediate results, but in long-term growth. Two years after I finished working with Jim, he reached out and said, "I just wanted to let you know that the top three clients I've ever had come from the outreach that we did, and each generated $20,000 in revenue through my relationship with them. I'm sure you would want to hear that, so I just wanted to let you know."

This was the kind of feedback that I dream of–it's a diamond in the rough that makes all the hard work and uncertainty worthwhile for me.

In the realm of coaching, a client's growth can manifest in a multitude of ways. It's usually a gradual, incremental expansion over time, but it can also be marked by a more immediate, substantial surge in clientele, revenue, and prestige.

To me, this is the essence of growth in coaching; an organic evolution, bolstered by a portfolio of achievements, and defined by an unwavering commitment to excellence.

TYSON KNAUF

Another client of mine named Maryanne started working with me last December, and she was incredibly easy to work with initially. However, as we began planning and putting together her program, we discovered that she only wanted to work with women and didn't want any men included in her outreach on LinkedIn.

Unfortunately, there's no gender filter on LinkedIn, so we had to come up with a solution. Even though Maryanne was a high-maintenance client, she was willing to work with me to find a way to make it happen.

So, I had my virtual assistant manually groom her outreach list by removing all the men so that only women were included.

In addition to her gender preferences, Maryanne also requested that all her messages be directed to her sales navigator inbox, as opposed to her regular LinkedIn inbox. This was because she didn't want her inbox to be cluttered with messages.

While this was difficult, I had previously used a different approach with other clients, marking important messages with a red flag. I thought that could be a solution at first, but Maryanne was insistent with her request.

After speaking with my IT guys, I found out that what Maryanne wanted was not an option with the software we were using at the time. So, my VAs took on the task of doing all the custom outreach while I researched a solution. Thankfully, I discovered a new software that not only met my client's expectations, but was also better than what I was using before.

Overall, my experience with Maryanne helped me find a better solution for my business, and I'm grateful for that. If I hadn't taken on her challenge, I wouldn't have discovered the program that has since replaced my old software, which, in hindsight, was starting to fall apart. The experience taught me a lot about flexibility and problem-solving in coaching.

It's truly remarkable how clients can help open up new opportunities, even in the midst of seemingly high-maintenance requests. But that can only happen if you have the right mindset.

Initially, Maryanne's requests were a hurdle for me, but then I was like, 'Let's see what else is out there.' Having been in this business for a while now, I'm tied to a group of other marketers, which means there is lots of intellectual capital that I can draw on to find solutions.

Instead of simply denying my client's unique needs, I chose to explore alternative solutions and, in doing so, uncovered a better software for my business. Through grace, you can view any situation not as a hurdle, but as an opportunity.

With such a perspective, even the most demanding clients can lead to unexpected and rewarding outcomes. She and I are actually still working together, which is really great.

With Maryanne, I found that her strictness was tempered by an unflaggingly positive attitude, a quality that proved indispensable during difficult times. Even when her feedback was critical, and her timelines were tight, she always managed to inspire optimism and encouragement.

For this reason, I seek out clients who are similarly direct, growth-driven, and positive. Such relationships allow for mutual support and grace in the face of challenges, including those related to mastering new software tools.

By openly sharing our struggles and obstacles, we can transcend mere transactions and forge more meaningful relationships. I think the best relationships are ones in which grace is extended to those involved throughout the process.

When I went to discover new software, Maryanne held out for me. Indeed, the process of personal growth requires us to embrace our vulnerabilities, much as tarantulas must do when molting or growing. Thus, by balancing confidence with vulnerability, we can achieve a powerful and productive dynamic in any interaction.

Vulnerability is a fundamental component of personal growth and relationship-building. Only by embracing our vulnerabilities and being willing to share them can we achieve truly profound connections that transcend the transactional.

Interestingly, this concept applies even to tarantulas, as they must display remarkable vulnerability during periods of molting and growth. Though seemingly incongruous, this parallel underscores the importance of confidence and vulnerability in all interactions.

Striking a balance between those two qualities can lead to a uniquely productive and impactful dynamic. Working with Maryanne amidst the uncertainty of doing something that could have landed me flat on my face, I found solace in my hope in the process, even though the risks of failure were high.

In my line of work, I am no stranger to navigating various software challenges. In fact, I have encountered four distinct ones over the past six years alone. And with each new challenge, I remained steadfast in my belief that there was always a way forward.

But what made all the difference on this occasion was the support system I had in place. After six years of building relationships in my industry, I have developed a robust network of like-minded professionals who are always willing to lend a helping hand.

I can literally just go into a few different Discord groups and say, "Hey, this is what I'm trying to accomplish. Does anyone know how to do x?" With their guidance, I was able to identify and settle on the best software solution for Maryanne with ease.

Whenever a client presents a challenge, I make it my personal mission to find a solution promptly. But I cannot afford to let this pursuit impede progress.

This is where my team comes in. Thankfully, I have a

capable staff that I can delegate tasks to while I focus on finding a solution.

Admittedly, I invested more time than usual on that project for Maryanne, but it was worth it.

In my experience, the key to success is having a diverse range of tools at your disposal. If I had relied on just one tool, I would have been forced to step back and reconsider my approach. But by being flexible and adaptable, we were able to stay the course and deliver the promised results to our client.

The essence of grace often lies in the company you keep. When you surround yourself with the right people, not only can you extend grace, but you can also receive and discover new opportunities.

It's like grace begets grace. Your close friends and long-term colleagues will share ideas and thoughts with you, extending their generosity.

Conversely, clients who are just getting to know you have to exercise more faith, relying on your expertise and judgment. The communal dynamic can make all the difference in a fast-paced marketplace, where nimbleness is key.

Having reliable people to turn to for advice, ideas, and support can empower you to navigate challenges with greater ease. It's akin to a beehive, where each member contributes to the greater good, fostering the spirit of collaboration and mutual benefit.

Vulnerability is an integral part of coaching, but it's important to find the right balance. When clients come to you with a problem, you should be honest with them about your limitations, but also show them that you're willing to go the extra mile to find a solution.

For instance, you could tell them that you don't have the software to help them right now, but you're confident that you can find a solution. It's important to be transparent about your process so that clients can appreciate the effort you're putting in.

As a coach, you should also strive to be vulnerable enough to help your clients understand your process, but not to the point where you're projecting your fears onto them. Instead, focus on lifting the hood and showing them what you're doing to get results.

Be willing to go the extra mile, but also set boundaries to protect your well-being. Remember, coaching is a partnership.

Sharing with my clients that I was writing this book was an act that inherently required a certain level of vulnerability. It's not every day that one admits to writing about their affinity for weird animals in the context of a book about business relationships. But, it becomes an easy bridge to establish deeper rapport.

This form of vulnerability is akin to personal relationship vulnerability, but one that lends itself well to fostering deeper professional connections.

Vulnerability comes in different forms. In personal relationships, it may mean opening up about the deeper aspects of oneself, what makes one tick, and what one likes or dislikes. With clients, however, it often takes the shape of process vulnerability, wherein the coach must be willing to expose their methods and approach to facilitate understanding and collaboration. Then clients will also be vulnerable in sharing their business details, goals, and obstacles.

I have learned that clients often take the first step in expressing their vulnerabilities. In our initial interactions, they're quick to lay out their current situation and aspirations. It is then up to me to reciprocate by being forthcoming about what matters to them, without necessarily sharing irrelevant details.

This exchange creates an opportunity to open our hearts to each other, working towards a mutual understanding. A successful partnership usually emerges when clients recognize my skill set, and I am able to offer guidance and ideas, while also taking into account their preferences and feedback.

My recent experiences have shown me that embracing vulnerability in my practice can lead to positive results. Collaborating with clients, being receptive to their ideas, and finding common ground has always borne fruitful outcomes for my business.

Hope in the Process

When approaching one of my tarantulas, I don't just scoop it onto my hand right away. I need to see where they're at, prod them a little bit, and see how they respond. Their response usually tells me if they are going to be grumpy or not.

This is much like how I approach a potential client. Both tasks require careful observation and the right approach in order to determine if it's safe to proceed. In the case of potential clients on LinkedIn, asking the right questions is crucial to determining their level of readiness and interest in your services.

It's also important to remember that not everyone will be ready for your services at the same time. Just like the tarantula may not be ready to come out of its cage, a potential client may not be ready to commit to working with you right away. However, by building trust and staying connected, you may be able to revisit the conversation at a later time when they are more open to the idea.

For example, I've just onboarded a new client. About a year and a half ago, I reached out to his business partner just after the lockdown happened. They were just figuring things out at the time, but they still had momentum. However, he informed me that my process was not what they were looking for and ended the conversation.

Despite this, we remained connected. Fast-forward a year and a half, and I ended up connecting with his partner on LinkedIn. I reached out to him, and he found what I had to offer interesting, so we set up a call.

What's funny is that this guy mentioned he was partners with Tim, the guy I had reached out to previously, but when I had first reached out to them, they had been in a completely different mindset and just weren't ready at the time.

I believe that using questions to respectfully and genuinely probe someone's mindset and intentions is key in testing the waters with potential clients, much like how I test the waters with tarantulas.

The process of building relationships is not a linear one, but rather an evolution of stages, as in Bruce Tuckman's 'forming, storming, norming and performing' model. By reframing challenges encountered as a necessary step in the process of building relationships, you can adopt a more optimistic outlook and recognize the bigger picture.

Rather than viewing difficulties as random or personal setbacks, understand that they are merely part of a larger journey. You have to think, 'This is happening now, but this is only one step.' Taking a process-oriented approach allows for a clearer understanding of where you are and where you're headed, while still being mindful of the present moment.

When clients express frustration or vulnerability, it presents an opportunity to engage in open communication and collaboration, which often leads to positive outcomes. The key is to maintain openness to new ideas and questions, and to approach the work with a spirit of 'grace for grace.'

I'm happy to accommodate someone's needs, as long as they're willing to allow me the creative freedom to do my best work. Allowing space for each other is crucial in navigating any challenges that may arise.

The most successful client relationships are built on trust, which can be fostered through genuine vulnerability and honesty. Rather than hiding fears or anxieties, acknowledging them and exploring potential roadblocks together can create a more authentic connection.

This doesn't necessarily mean outlining specific fears, but rather identifying potential obstacles and considering them collaboratively. By fostering this kind of open communication, clients are more likely to feel confident in my abilities and trust my expertise.

I prioritize being available to my clients and their ideas, without ever making them feel like I don't have time for them. If I can't give them my full attention at a certain moment, I'll let them know when I have time, whether that's later in the day or the next day.

By giving them the space to discuss and ask questions, we can work together to come up with solutions. Collaboration is key, as opposed to a top-down approach where I dictate solutions to them.

To achieve this collaborative dynamic, I take a 'brain ninja' approach where I don't immediately dismiss any idea, but instead try to understand it better. By asking questions and inviting a client to contribute their own ideas, we can build a relationship that is not one-sided.

This is especially important when working with challenging clients, such as one recent addition to my roster. She presented some communication challenges, but I personally did not find them to be a hindrance.

The client had previously been let go by her former digital marketer, leading her to initially question her own capabilities. But as we worked together, these doubts eventually subsided, and she expressed appreciation for our collaborative approach.

As I grow my business, I acknowledge that there may be a temptation to be picky about the people I choose to work with. However, I think it's important to establish a relationship with clients early on and not be overly selective after the fact.

When clients share their vulnerabilities with me, it's a sign of trust that I value deeply and will respect going forward. These types of interactions make my work meaningful and fulfilling.

Surround Yourself with the Right People

Assembling the right people around you is akin to the delicate art of handling tarantulas. In my experience, when I approach a tarantula, it will either turn towards me with aggression, or it will corral, allowing me to move it around with ease.

But if it starts out aggressive, I can actually change its disposition to non-aggressive by calmly getting it to move around until it eventually calms down enough to be picked up.

With people, the process is much the same. You must gently prod them, asking them where they are and what they hope to accomplish in order to establish a strong foundation for the relationship. By recognizing not only opportunities for others but also areas in which they can help you, you can build a powerful network of engaged professionals.

On LinkedIn, I spend my days prodding people, engaging with them one-on-one in order to build a network of truly connected individuals. This approach has allowed me to create a network of people with whom I am actually engaged, rather than simply being 'connected.'

As I get to know people, I gain an understanding of their strengths and reservations, which allows me to help them or seek their help accordingly. When opportunities arise, I can turn to someone in my network and know that they are someone I can trust to help me or connect me with the right person.

Over time, business relationships happen organically as we give and receive opportunities.

When building your network, it is important to view relationships as opportunities for both giving and receiving. Consider what opportunities you can send someone's way, or how you can connect them with someone else in your network.

This requires a long-term view, rather than simply seeking immediate gratification. By looking far down the road, you can build a powerful network that will serve you well in the years to come.

Vulnerable Enough to Help

There's a certain power in vulnerability, a power that can make people feel at ease and more willing to open up. When they see that you're vulnerable, they feel more inclined to be vulnerable. When we let our guard down and shed our armor, it creates a sense of intimacy and connection that is hard to come by otherwise.

It's a recognition that we don't have to perfect all the time. It is being able to create a greater sense of intimacy in relationships like, "I'm not going to be defensive with you, I know that you've got my back."

For many of us, vulnerability can be a scary prospect. We fear rejection or ridicule, so we put up walls to protect ourselves. But when we do that, we're cutting ourselves off from the potential of experiencing deep, meaningful relationships.

We're missing out on the opportunity to connect with others on a more authentic level. When it came to working with my client Maryanne, I was like, "I don't have the answer now, but I know I've got enough buttons to push that I can get the answer."

That's why vulnerability is so important. It's not about blindly trusting others and hoping for the best. It's about having faith in the people we've surrounded ourselves with, knowing that they have our back and we have theirs.

It's like crowd-surfing–you need to trust that there are people there to catch you if you fall. And if you've built strong relationships based on mutual trust and respect, you can be vulnerable without fear.

Of course, vulnerability isn't a magic solution to all our problems. It's not a guarantee that everything will work out perfectly. But it is a way to create a space where we can connect more deeply with others. A space where we can build stronger relationships based on mutual trust and respect.

The notion of vulnerability has taken me off the lofty pedestal that once seemed enticing, but ultimately proved too precarious to remain atop. Keeping oneself perched high above one's clients creates a perpetual need to maintain that elevated status.

However, being on a pedestal doesn't necessarily equate to producing results. The results should speak for themselves, without the need for embellishment or puffery. It's about focusing on the outcomes, which is the crux of the matter.

For instance, if we didn't achieve the desired results for a client this week, it's about saying, "Here are the reasons why, and here is what we intend to change to ensure success."

Or, if we achieved the desired results, "Here are the factors that contributed to our success, and here is what we intend to maintain going forward."

The emphasis should be on the results rather than on the image. While having a positive image is crucial, there comes a point where it can become excessive.

But I don't think there are steps you can follow to make it magically happen. You just have to learn to be comfortable with vulnerability and embrace it whole-heartedly.

When working with clients, there's always a risk of negative feedback or uncertainty. However, if you are comfortable with yourself, it sets the tone for the entire interaction.

Building up one's tolerance to discomfort can enable one to assist clients in developing their own tolerance levels. This, in turn, allows them to step outside of their comfort zones and explore new possibilities without fear, trusting in themselves and others. That's a huge thing for me.

The clients I collaborate with best are those who trust me. They know that I have their best interests at heart and that I will do everything within my power to achieve the outcomes we discussed. If things are not going well, they will be made aware of it promptly, rather than discovering it later down the road.

I believe that vulnerability and trust are intertwined.

Being vulnerable does not necessitate stripping oneself of all defenses. Rather, it requires being comfortable and confident enough to share one's thought process with clients when appropriate and to involve them in the process. This, I believe, is the key ingredient.

My role is to leverage all my expertise and generate results. However, when combined with the knowledge of my clients, the outcome is greater than the sum of its parts. By bringing together their insights with mine, we create a unique, more powerful offering than we could produce alone.

This approach resonates with clients, as they feel engaged in the process and empowered to contribute to it. They appreciate the fact that I am saving them time while still allowing them to have a say. It's a winning combination, in my view.

Vulnerability breeds vulnerability, which in turn stimulates deeper relationships. In these connections, we can cultivate growth by extending grace and accepting it in return.

Grace is the essence of an environment that allows for mistakes to be made and embraced, for falls to be dusted off, and for people to get back up and try again.

By bestowing grace upon others, we create a space where we too can receive it, recognizing that none of us are perfect, but that we are all striving towards self-improvement.

In relationships, it is vital that we allow ourselves to be vulnerable, take risks, and grow. By extending the benefit of the doubt to others, we open the door for that to happen.

The freedom to pursue what we are best at is a fundamental human desire, and it can only be fulfilled in an atmosphere of trust and grace. These two concepts are intimately connected, and they form the very bedrock of genuine relationships and meaningful growth.

I think grace is the ultimate enabler of growth. It affords you the freedom to expand and evolve, unfettered by the constraints of perfection.

Growth does not thrive in an environment where everything proceeds according to plan; that is merely success without the possibility of improvement. Grace, on the other hand, in combination with meekness, provides a space to be vulnerable without fear of annihilation.

Consider the tarantula, ensconced in its protective habitat, able to be vulnerable without being devoured. Similarly, grace allows you to make mistakes and learn and grow from them, without fear of retribution or recrimination.

From a religious standpoint, grace represents the profound realization that even our best efforts are not enough, and that grace is the counterbalance to our shortcomings. It is the fuel that motivates us to keep moving forward and striving for improvement.

Paradoxically, to become more perfect, we must embrace our imperfections, for it is through grace that we can learn and grow. And, in turn, we must offer grace to others, recognizing that it is both a gift received and given.

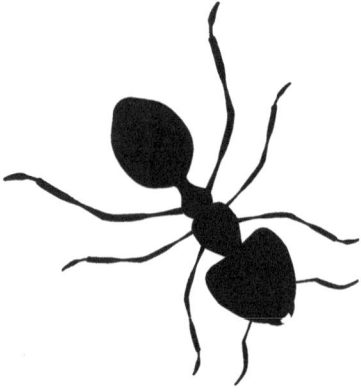

Chapter 4

Ant Bully

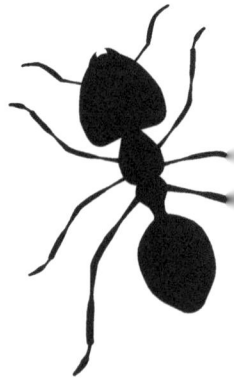

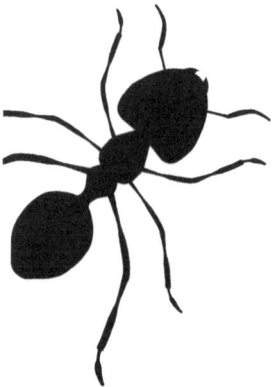

C hildren are curious explorers by nature, and their inquisitiveness leads them to explore and interact with the world around them. As they explore, they may engage in some harmful activities because they don't understand the full consequences of their actions. But through exposure and experience, children can gradually develop their understanding of what is right and what is wrong.

In the business world, creating an environment that fosters curiosity and exploration leads to new ideas, products, and services. When we nurture our natural curiosity and inquisitiveness, it can lead to a more vibrant and innovative business ecosystem.

When I was younger, I was curious about the behavior of ants, and I spent hours observing them closely. I also enjoyed conducting experiments on them, which, unfortunately, sometimes involved causing harm and being cruel.

Although my methods were not always ethical, I was driven by curiosity, and I was trying to figure out how the world worked.

My childhood experimentation with ants involved pulling off their heads quite a lot. There were also these large red and black ants around my house, and I would get them to bite a rose thorn, and then I would decorate a whole rose branch with them.

Sometimes, I would capture two ants and put them at either end of one of the clear vegetable capsules that my mom had. I would use a magnifying glass to focus the sunlight on one end of the capsule to burn one ant. Then the smoke from the burning would suffocate the ant at the other end.

I also carried out more innocent experiments. I would put a bunch of ants in mud, and it would harden them into statues. When mud dries up, it's porous, so they could still breathe through the clay. Then I would pour water on them, and they would come back to life and scamper away.

Unfortunately, my cruel experiments did not stop with ants.

Every now and then, I would burn a hairspray circle around a slug and then light it on fire. I would also bully spiders by capturing them and forcing them to bite each other.

In one particularly disturbing incident, I even used an air gun to shoot my sister with a centipede, which she still reminds me of to this day.

I have often wondered about my fascination with subjecting small insects to cruel experiments as a child. Perhaps some of it was derived from a sense of power that it gave me.

However, I also think that much of it was due to my ignorance. I lacked an understanding of the suffering I was causing.

Like many children, I treated insects more like playthings or robots rather than living beings. My childhood ignorance failed to grasp the consequences of my actions.

Looking back, I recognize the disturbing nature of these actions, and sometimes I wonder if I was exhibiting the early signs of psychopathic tendencies!

Now, I am incredibly grateful that my childhood experiences did not lead me down a path toward more violent behavior as an adult.

Although my fascination with these cruel experiments was initially driven by curiosity, I cannot deny the harm that I caused. I now feel bad for my childhood actions, and this has led me to develop a deep passion for conservation and a greater appreciation of the interconnectedness of all living things.

Those early experiences with ants actually sparked a lifelong passion for science and discovery in me. That passion has led me to continue educating myself and helped me grow into a more compassionate and aware individual.

Over the years, my perspective began to shift. I recall interacting with my uncle from England, who had the extreme opposite approach to insects. He was the kind of person who would catch a mosquito and then release it outside.

During a visit one summer, he encountered a tick on someone's skin. It hadn't bitten the person yet, and before anyone could react, he scooped it up and went out to set it free instead of killing it. At the time, I thought he was a complete weirdo, but I think seeing him act differently toward insects helped me to begin shifting my perspective.

As I grew older and learned more about nature, I began to appreciate the intricacy and diversity of the natural world.

I came to realize that insects weren't my playthings, and they had a vital role in our ecosystem. These small beings were actually rather sophisticated living creatures with unique abilities and personalities.

I think I became much more empathetic.

At first, it was simply a matter of understanding that these insects could feel pain. This realization began to erode my willingness to conduct experiments that caused them harm.

It was replaced with a sense of responsibility for the well-being of these creatures. I'm glad, however, that my curiosity stuck with me, and I remained intrigued by their complexity and individuality.

I was about 13 or 14 years old when I adopted a pair of Madagascar Hissing Cockroaches. They were my first pet bugs, and I believe it wasn't until then that I think my relationship with insects truly shifted.

As I observed them in their new environment, I began to see them not as playthings, but as creatures deserving of care and attention. I watched as they developed, mated, and had these little clutches of cockroaches.

Seeing how they started their own family, I started to relate with them more in terms of what I was going through.

I realized that they were growing just as I was growing, and I noticed a pattern of behavior in them that indicated intelligence and adaptability. And maybe that was the catalyst for me.

It all came down to recognizing that there was intelligence in these insects that I had not seen before.

As I grew older, I began to see insects more as individuals rather than mere cogs in a machine. I began to recognize their value and respect their place within our larger ecosystem.

My growing empathy for my insects, particularly ants, led me to understand more about them. It allowed me to move beyond my initial fascination with their uniqueness and gain a deeper appreciation of their value and importance to the planet's delicate balance.

As time passed, and I spent more time scrutinizing their way of life, I began to see a different side to these tiny creatures and how they all acted differently.

From my perspective, they started to emerge as distinct individuals, each with their own unique personality and approach to life.

It was a revelation, and I realized that my previous perceptions about them were misguided. Ants were far more complex and nuanced than I had ever imagined.

With that realization came a newfound respect and appreciation for these remarkable creatures.

When I began to keep ants and more insects as pets, I was able to observe them more closely in a confined environment, and I began to understand their needs and behaviors.

Before, I just saw them as little more than pre-programmed creatures and mere cogs in the hive's wheel. It was easy to strip them of any individuality or agency and view them as expendable, disposable beings.

But in observing them, I began to see parallels between myself and them and started appreciating the interconnectedness of all living things and the symbiotic relationships that exist within nature.

For instance, I was fascinated by the way red and black ants would carry other live ants as if they were royalty. I started recognizing similar patterns in society and realized that there's a lot of intelligence in insect behavior and their societal structures that can easily be overlooked.

That was like the first thread of tying myself to these creatures, and I began to see them in a new light.

The complexity of it all became the foundation for which I began to develop a passion for exploring and discovering their world.

As I learned more about ants and insect behavior, I found myself taking less joy in killing them. It wasn't an immediate change, and I didn't quit cold turkey, rather it was a gradual shift in perspective.

Instead of seeing them as mere playthings, I began to recognize the humanity in insects.

One memory that stands out for me is a spring day when my mother and I watched as male ants took flight in search of mates.

There is one species of male ant with wings that emerge from their colonies all around the world on certain days of the year. They flap their wings in the air, and if it's sunny, and you look at the right angle, you'll see patches up in the sky where their wings catch the sun.

Similarly, I discovered that male bees will fly up to mate with a female who has emitted a pheromone. As they circle around her, they'll form patches in the air. This phenomenon occurs on specific days throughout the year and is such a fascinating wonder of nature to see.

As I became more curious, I shifted from being a hands-on torturer to a patient and curious observer of insects. I wanted to learn more, to understand more, and to appreciate more.

Nowadays, my mom always says to me, "You notice things in nature that people don't really notice."

And so, my journey of discovery continues, fueled by a deepening appreciation for the complexity of the natural world.

Pain Sparks Empathy and Connection

I can trace my journey of appreciating nature back to one pivotal realization and discovery: 'These tiny creatures called ants feel pain, just as I do.'

Recognizing that something so different from me could still experience something as personal as pain was quite profound.

Discovering the universality of pain, and recognizing other similarities between myself and ants, was significant in the development of my passion for nature.

It was about noticing relatable characteristics and seeing things in nature that I understood in myself. Or seeing things in nature that I didn't understand, but were amazing.

When I first observed flying ant patches in the sky, it was initially a phenomenon to me until further examination of bee behavior shed light on what was happening in their world, and how ants and bees are kind of related that way.

Witnessing pain in humans or animals triggers empathy to kick in, and this can be a starting point for understanding and compassion.

For example, research on motor neurons in the brain suggests that when we see someone experiencing pain, our own pain centers are activated, leading us to feel sympathetic pain.

Pain is a universal experience that can help us relate to others. Witnessing pain in humans or animals triggers empathy to kick in. You can't see someone fall down the stairs and not feel sympathetic pain. It feels to me like pain is a starting point for empathy and understanding.

This is evident in nature as well. Animals are capable of displaying empathetic behavior toward their own kind as well as toward other species. Take, for example, the incident captured on video where a child fell into a gorilla enclosure. Rather than attacking the child, the gorillas in the pen actually displayed a remarkable level of empathy and protective behavior, surrounding and guarding the child. They appeared to recognize the child's vulnerability and responded with care and concern.

When people entered the enclosure to rescue the child, the gorillas calmly moved out of the way, allowing the humans to take over.

However, the situation ended tragically as one of the gorillas was shot and killed by the guards. It was particularly heartbreaking for many as the gorilla was not displaying any aggressive behavior.

This incident shows us the importance of approaching interactions with animals in a cautious and empathetic manner. While it is crucial to ensure the safety of other humans, it is also essential to recognize the intelligence and emotional capacity of animals and treat them with respect and compassion.

How those gorillas behaved is a great reminder that nature, including human nature, has an innate ability to empathize with pain.

The capacity to feel another's pain is a fundamental starting point for understanding and appreciating a person. When we can empathize with someone's pain, we establish a connection. By understanding what another living thing is going through, we gain insight into their experience, and we are better equipped to offer support and compassion.

Discovering Life Through Pain

I don't recall a specific moment when I realized that insects, like ants, could feel pain, but I began to empathize with them over time as I observed them. I saw how they acted similarly to me and how they can get injured, experience hurt, and struggle for quite a while.

The capacity for pain perception among insects, including ants, has been a topic of scientific inquiry for many years. There is a growing body of evidence that suggests they do, in fact, possess the neurological structures necessary to process painful stimuli.

As I continued to observe the behavior of ants, I began to understand that my actions could cause them pain.

This realization led to me gaining empathy, and I gradually just stopped doing things that hurt them. Instead, I shifted my focus to observing them and became fascinated by their locomotion, movement, and intelligence, both on an individual and collective level.

They have a remarkable ability to communicate with each other and coordinate complex behaviors, including the management of injured and sick colony members, suggesting that not only do they have a capacity for pain perception, but they also have a level of empathy for their fellow colony members.

Pain is a unifying factor that connects us all together in business. It really is. Empathy for other people's pain allows us to better understand the needs and experiences of those we are seeking to help professionally.

Without empathy, we risk creating solutions that do not truly meet the needs of the people we aim to cater to or serve.

As human beings, we have the capacity to feel empathy, which allows us to understand and relate to others' experiences of pain. If we fail to empathize with others who are undergoing pain, we might not be in a position to provide the relief, support, or comfort needed to alleviate their suffering.

In many cases, pain can be a unifying factor that enables individuals to connect with each other and create a sense of community.

Painful experiences can be used as catalysts to prompt

individuals to seek out others who may have gone through similar experiences and form a support system.

Without empathy, the connection is lost, and it's difficult to help others. Empathy is essential in building meaningful relationships because to have it requires being open to learning and growth, which allows us to gain deeper insights into others' experiences and needs.

In the business world, there are some who might be considered "ant bullies." People who are still in their ant-bully phase have no empathy and look at other people without regard for their feelings.

These individuals approach problem-solving and offer solutions in a way that is aggressive and often causes more harm than good.

However, I have rarely encountered ant bullies in the business world–and I do a lot of outreach.

I have probably reached out to close to a million people in the last six years, and I've only had a handful of people that kind of cursed me out.

Occasionally, when I reach out to people on LinkedIn or through other channels, I may come across a person who is unresponsive or even hostile, but I don't see them as a bully per se.

It could be that they are just not interested in what I have to offer, or I simply caught them on the wrong day.

I try not to take it personally and move on. I understand that people's reactions can be influenced by a variety of factors, such as past experiences, prior interactions, or current circumstances. Therefore, I don't judge them based on a single encounter and give them the benefit of the doubt.

I don't deny the existence of ant bullies in the professional world, but they are few and far between.

Those who are young, aggressive, experimental, and still figuring out things, driven mostly by curiosity without regard for others, are definitely out there. But, as people mature, empathy kicks in, and we learn to filter.

That empathetic approach is crucial when it comes to interacting with others in business. If you come across as overly aggressive or dismissive of others' opinions, then you're going to come across as an ant bully. Or worse, you'll uncover bigger bullies, and they'll come after you.

Interacting with others is similar to handling animals–if you understand their behavior and limits, you can avoid provoking them. Similarly, by observing people carefully, you can learn to interact with them effectively and avoid triggering their aggression.

In my experience, ant bullies tend to lack empathy due to a lack of diverse experiences in their lives. Empathy is essential in understanding others and building productive relationships. As such, one can say that becoming empathetic is key to avoiding becoming an ant bully.

By seeking to understand others and putting yourself in

their shoes, you can build rapport and trust, which are critical to success in business.

If someone doesn't have experiences that force them to find empathy in their life, then they're more likely to remain an ant bully.

In other words, without making an effort to discover new people and new experiences, you risk being the ant bully. Don't let that happen.

Empathizing with Life

Empathy is a powerful tool that allows us to understand and connect with others on a deeper level. For me, the first step in empathizing with ants was recognizing that they were not just mindless robots, but rather individuals who help each other.

Seeing one ant carry another one was a revelation for me, and it made me wonder what else they were capable of that I had missed up to then. It kind of stuck with me.

I thought, 'Why would an ant do that?' Then the 'why' started to grow in my mind.

Over time, I began to see that ants were not only willing to help each other, but they were also ready to sacrifice themselves for their community. When I witnessed their bravery and selflessness, it was awe-inspiring for me.

As a child, I was always drawn to those who were strong and brave, and I found myself relating to ants in that way. If you ever touch an ant hive, you won't see them running back into their holes and hiding. The guards will come out, and they're badass, man.

They're committed to the end. And they don't just sit back with their guns and shoot like we do–they go all in, face-first.

Ants are not only willing to help each other, but they are also willing to sacrifice themselves, without hesitation, for the greater good.

Their level of commitment and determination is truly admirable. They confront their attackers head-on, using their bodies as shields. This kind of bravery and self-sacrifice is something that I can relate to.

The complexity of nature, as seen in ants, has always fascinated me and really stuck with me over the years. The more I look at nature and ants, the more I realize how intricate and multifaceted their societies are.

During a visit to the Victoria Bug Zoo on Vancouver Island, I saw an ant colony up close for the first time. The colony had different boxes for waste and fungus gardens, which were nourished by the leaves the ants collected.

The ants didn't eat the leaves but used them as fertilizer for growing fungus which they consumed. Seeing the level of organization and strategy of these leaf-cutter ants was mind-blowing. I realized that even in the smallest creatures, there are echoes of human society.

Once you start to see the echoes, or as physicist Edward Witten puts it, "the rhymes in nature," you begin to see things like ant colonies as one part of a greater whole that you can relate to and with.

Empathy is a powerful tool that leads to understanding, especially when it comes to pain. Understanding someone's pain is the first step toward helping them. When we empathize with others, we feel their pain and their desire to alleviate it.

Conversely, when someone empathizes with us, we feel understood, which makes us more receptive to receiving help. Pain is such a common human experience that when we see strangers in pain, we are drawn to help them. It's this shared experience that brings us closer as a community and as human beings.

If you're walking down the street, and you see someone on the side of the street in pain, often your first thought will be, 'What's wrong? What's happening?'

That's the first draw, from stranger to stranger, it's being able to recognize and empathize with pain.

Cross-Pollination of Intelligence

When I reflect on ants' behavior, it is fascinating to see how they exhibit similarities to our societies.

In a business sense, cross-pollination occurs when ideas, thoughts, and strategies are exchanged, leading to the discovery of new leads and opportunities. Creating an environment that fosters the sharing and hearing of ideas is vital to enable cross-pollination.

The cross-pollination of ideas comes from being able to create an environment where you can both share what you think and be heard.

When I started out in my business, I had to learn to listen, to be comfortable with silence, and to let people talk.

Listening is a critical aspect of my business, as it allows individuals to express their thoughts and feelings. It also allows me to ask them the right questions that will give them the canvas to express their feelings.

By asking the right questions and observing, we can recognize the thought processes of others. Often, brilliant ideas come from a space where individuals feel heard and appreciated. Thus, cross-pollination of intelligence is essential to promoting growth and development.

Usually, brilliance comes from an environment where people can express ideas and be heard.

In that setting, it is also easier to empathize with others and recognize the ways in which you can help them.

As individuals, we tend to work alone, similar to ants. But like ants, who can only survive on their own for so long, we cannot survive in isolation.

We're much the same as ants in that if we don't cross-pollinate and share our intelligence and ideas with others, we will slowly die.

In the business world, this exchange of knowledge is critical to success. If businesses fail to bring in new team members, provide ongoing training and development, and explore new ideas and approaches, they risk becoming stagnant.

This stagnation can be as detrimental, like moving backward, as competitors continue to innovate and adapt.

The lesson we can learn from ants is clear: by working with others, you can accomplish far more than you ever could on your own.

Relating to Behavior

Ants are cool creatures that offer a unique perspective on society and human behavior. They are highly accessible and easy to study, making them an ideal model for understanding the complexities of social organization and cooperation. There's pure intelligence to them in a lot of ways.

Through observing ants, we can gain valuable insights into human nature and the ways in which we interact with each other. Ants are not so different from us in many ways, and their behavior can serve as a reflection of our own.

It is remarkable how they possess a level of collective intelligence that allows them to work together in incredibly efficient and effective ways. Their self-sacrificing behavior and bravery in the face of danger serve as a testament to the power of teamwork and cooperation.

If you never take the time to sit and observe the natural world around you, you will miss out on the beauty of life.

For me, ants were the first building blocks in seeing that beauty. I had to learn to observe closely, and in doing so, I discovered a world of wonder that I had never appreciated before.

Unfortunately, we don't observe nearly enough in our lives. Our busy lives prevent us from slowing down to take in the beauty that surrounds us, and we get caught up in the everyday grind and forget to appreciate the present.

The same is true when it comes to people. If we take the time to observe them closely, we can gain a deeper understanding of their unique perspectives and experiences.

We overlook the richness of human interaction when we see others as mere objects or obstacles in our path. There are endless things we don't have to miss, we just have to take the time to sit and observe. I think we forget what we came here for.

As I reflect on my journey, from ant bully to observer, I am struck by how powerful observation can be in creating opportunities, particularly in business.

Years ago, I heard a saying that stuck with me: "If you learn more about people than your products or services, you'll become unusually successful."

I recently realized that people don't just buy my service, they buy me, and they buy what I have been able to observe in them. This has led me to become more empathetic in observing people, both clients and prospective clients, in order to recognize ways in which we can create opportunities.

I've learned to shift from acting on things impulsively to observing things before acting.

The skill has helped me tremendously in my interactions with people. It's about taking a moment to observe and really see what's going on, rather than jumping to conclusions based on assumptions or preconceptions.

By doing so, I have been able to better understand and connect with those around me, thus creating opportunities for growth and success.

To move from being an ant bully to an observer, I believe the first step is to learn to empathize. Empathy goes a long way. It's not just a matter of recognizing pain or struggle, it's also about curiosity.

Curiosity fuels observation, and by being genuinely interested in others, we can naturally observe and learn from them.

When I was younger, I thought I knew everything, and I always acted without understanding. That's essentially what an ant bully is: someone who acts or reacts without understanding.

On the other hand, observation and empathy have taught me that there is always more to learn and understand about others.

It's about helping others recognize and appreciate the things that they have, and being part of a supportive community where everyone can grow and succeed together. It's not about trying to do it alone.

In my experience, developing empathy towards others starts with recognizing the pain and struggles they go through.

By taking the time to seek understanding before reacting, we can shift from a mindset that is dismissive of other people's experiences to one that is truly caring about the well-being of others.

While there may not be a lot of true ant bullies out there, they do exist. They may be more prevalent on certain platforms where anonymity is more common or where standards of behavior are not clearly established.

However, on professional platforms like LinkedIn, where reputation is important, there tends to be a lot less bullying behavior.

When we walk outside and see an ant crawling on the ground, we could easily step on it without a second thought. But if we take a closer look, we might begin to appreciate its tiny movements and its intricate design.

Similarly, if we pause and observe the people around us, we might begin to see their unique qualities and understand their experiences in a deeper way. We should all make a conscious effort to stop and look rather than mindlessly walk by.

The key is recognizing the pain that people go through and allowing it to stir empathy in us. That's how we avoid becoming an ant bully who crushes everything around us without a second thought.

Let us pause and truly see the ants on the ground.

Quit walking on them, and stop long enough to really seek an understanding first.

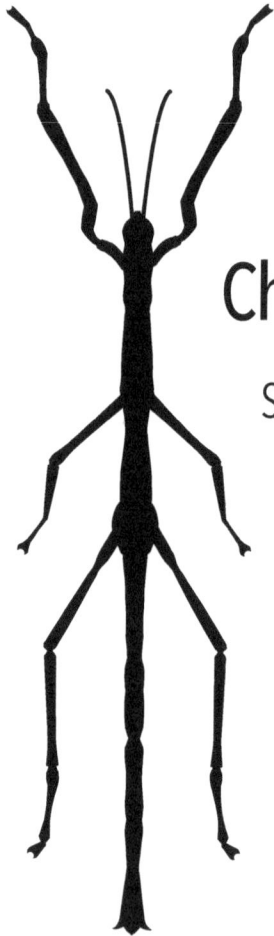

Chapter 5

Stick Bugs

W hen I was younger, my brother's biology teacher had a pet stick bug.

Though I never actually saw it, my brother always told me about it because of my interest in insects and other creatures.

I remember he would describe it as being a really big one, and he'd tell me how it would walk around. Just knowing that you could keep a stick bug as a pet seemed really cool to me back then.

Before that, I hadn't realized that you could actually get exotic bugs in Canada. When I found out, I wanted to have one too.

So I did some research and found a website called petbugs.com. It was started by this young kid out in New York, and the business is actually still alive, but they don't really use the site anymore.

I discovered the website was this amazing place that brought people together to buy and sell bugs. Though I actually didn't end up buying a stick bug from the site, I did get several other bugs from there.

My first real encounter with stick bugs was when I was in Germany as a missionary. I was living in Giessen, a university town with lots of students hanging around.

In my time there, I came across four biology students who all lived in the same dorm. They had a big terrarium with blackberry leaves growing inside. And it was full of stick bugs.

Similar to when I learned that my brother's biology teacher had a stick bug, I thought this was really cool.

These guys offered to give me two eggs, and I took them back to my shared apartment in the town. I took a little clear film container, put it over the eggs, and kept them by the window for a little while.

Both of them hatched, but only one made it out. The other egg kind of hardened before the stick bug got out because it wasn't humid enough in the container.

So, then I had this one stick bug that I named Ralph.

When you're a missionary in Germany, you travel around in pairs, which means you and your companion work together and live together. So, after the egg hatched, my companion and I ended up having this little pet in the window, which kept getting bigger.

I ended up moving our new pet to a different area later on, next to a vase with a blackberry branch growing in it. Ralph would just sit there next to the vase every day because he was happy to have food easily available.

My companion had a very hairy arm, and every time we had Ralph climb onto his arm, it would lay an egg. Stick bugs arc their tails like scorpions when laying an egg, and then they flick it off. And Ralph kept doing this on my companion's arm. It was very weird, and we just thought it was the funniest thing ever.

Years later, I found out why this happened. It turns out that stick bugs will lay eggs when they're on an animal. They'll flick their eggs off to get them on the animal's feathers or hair, so they can carry them further abroad.

So that's how they spread themselves out, by flicking their eggs on hairy things. Learning that was so funny. Ralph had been looking for an opportunity to spread and took it when it came.

Another thing about stick bugs is that they propagate like crazy. It's not the easiest thing to manage, and it was especially difficult when I was traveling in Germany.

I carried around this little stick bug container with all these eggs and babies in it, and I gave them to friends. It became a natural tendency of mine to offer people stick bug eggs. All the people I knew in Germany were getting them. I was like the Johnny Appleseed of stick bugs.

When I finally went back to Canada, I took some eggs with me, so I could keep some of the bugs at home.

A stick bug's body is about as long as a pencil, but its legs are about as long as three pencils. And I ended up having thousands of them.

When you keep them, you have to control their numbers. It's quite easy to do. When they lay their eggs, they just fall to the ground, so you can find them when you clean their cages. Then you can freeze the eggs, or you can let them hatch.

I gave away some of them to people, but I also started selling them to people who had chameleons. Chameleons love to eat stick bugs, and they only eat greens, so it's a really good, nutritious meal for them. I think I made over a thousand bucks one year just selling stick bugs to a few friends who had chameleons.

One time I went to a family reunion, and my cousin Kailin was there. I knew he'd love my stick bugs because he had a pet praying mantis when we were kids, and he's always been into that stuff. So I brought him down to show him my collection, and I ended up giving him a stick bug to take home.

We lost touch for a couple of years until we got back in contact last year, and he told me, "Yeah, they're propagating, and now all my friends in Vancouver have stick bugs!"

You could compare their behavior to the spread of ideas. When you have something that's interesting enough to spread, it's like wildfire.

I had to get rid of my stick bugs when I moved to Alberta because we don't have blackberries growing year round here. A lot of warmer areas, such as Kelowna, do, and that provides a food source for the bugs.

Now a friend from back home has my old colony, and from what I hear, they're continuing to grow like crazy.

Male stick bugs are very uncommon. They are brown and skinny and usually infertile. So the species is nearly all female, and they just clone themselves over and over again. They're kind of like bananas in that way.

I always wondered what would happen if a disease spread amongst them, but they seem to be doing just fine, spreading all over the place.

What I like most about stick bugs is that they do not look like an insect when you see them at first.

When they're walking, when they're settling into a place, they actually take their arms, and they spread them out in front of them. They'll align their head and antennas and the rest of their body to make themselves look like a branch.

They do this funny thing where they'll sit there and sway back and forth. It's the gnarliest thing to see. They do the same thing when they're walking. They're always swaying to make themselves look like a stick or a plant moving in the breeze.

They blend into nature so well. Even when I used to feed one to my chameleons, at first, they wondered what I was giving them. They would think it's a stick, but once they tasted it, they always wanted more.

Spread Like Wildfire

What I find fascinating about the stick bug species is that it started with just one egg. But what hatched from that egg ended up spreading its eggs onto tons and tons of animals. Then more and more stick bugs came into being. And eventually, they became people's pets.

It's neat how it just started from that one simple egg. I think it speaks of taking opportunities.

When I think about my old stick bug Ralph, it always laid an egg when it saw an opportunity. It wouldn't lay an egg on my arm because I wasn't hairy enough. But it saw an opportunity on my friend's arm.

In life, it's important to take the right opportunity to spread an idea or a thought when it presents itself.

Ralph recognized my friend's hairy arm, saw the opportunity, and took it. You'd think a stick bug would be the dumbest thing ever. But it's pretty brilliant in a way. Or at least it's programmed pretty brilliantly to do that.

People talk about multiplication in nature, but when you actually see it in a colony, you think, 'Whoa, holy cow!' I once ran a chart of how often my old stick bugs were laying eggs. They were laying about four eggs a day on average, and their hatch rate was about 60% to 75%.

So if you get four or five adults, and the eggs take about 30 days to hatch, you're pulling in thousands of these creatures every month. The quick multiplication aspect of stick bugs is pretty gnarly.

You don't always have to invent something new in business. Sometimes you just have to do more of the same thing.

The stick bug is kind of an example of that. It's not creating something new or better. It just creates more of the same.

It's kind of like the "If it ain't broke, don't fix it" mentality. It just replicates in mass, and it starts to spread like wildfire on its own.

We live in a world that's all about original ideas and thinking, and sometimes you can kind of get lost in that concept of 'I need to come up with something new and different.' And that's not always the case.

In my marketing, I once made a video about how to build trust with executives through LinkedIn. When I first watched it, I thought, 'It's not that great. It's pretty much stuff everyone knows already.'

It was about how to approach and talk to executives based on finding commonalities between you and them, and then engaging them on that when you find an opportunity to do so.

You might say, "Yeah, I really liked your posts. I like what you did. Here's something I've been talking to my audience about recently," or "Here's an idea or a thought that I had to put into a video, can I send it over to you to check out?"

I was being like a stick bug in making that video because the idea of building trust with executives on LinkedIn is a pretty standard idea. I didn't think it was that great of a video, but I had spent like a month working on it because I wanted to do it end to end without any clips. It took me forever, and it was a bit of grilling to do.

But I got it out, and I ended up getting about five or six clients just from it alone. I was shocked. I thought, 'Really? That actually worked?'

Sometimes I think we get so lost in trying to come up with something new that we forget that the standard thing, whatever is used in mass, can be just as good, if not sometimes better. Or we might sit on an idea for so long that we miss the opportunity to spread it because we don't think it's good enough.

Don't judge your thoughts or ideas; let the market decide if they're good or not. Don't let yourself decide if they're good enough. If you determine that, you're going to miss out on a lot of opportunities.

You should always be casting seeds into the market. If we don't cast ideas out into the marketplace, we'll never know what the potential is for our idea. So don't hold back your seeds!

You have to think of ideas as infinite and not hesitate to send your ideas and content to the market. If you're doing that, then your business will grow.

You must always look for opportunities to share your ideas. Don't just look for opportunities to come up with a brilliant idea.

If you see the right opportunity to share it, an idea doesn't have to be brilliant. But if the timing is brilliant, then you've got something that's valuable to others.

A toothbrush, at the right time, could be really great for someone. A toothbrush is nothing spectacular, but if you give it to someone at the right time and recognize the opportunity to share it, that is where real growth happens.

When I made that marketing video, I shared it with a lot of people I had identified as worth engaging with in terms of my business.

I started out in the video by detailing my LinkedIn profile; I gave some background on who I was and what got me into my line of work.

Then I went into saying, "Here are some of the things I have found recently when it comes to building relationships."

Even at the time, I knew the idea behind it was pretty basic, and I had a few people respond to it like, "Oh, that's nothing new." But then I would ask them, "Okay, well, what are you working on?" So I turned it into this other opportunity to connect with the people who didn't think my idea was that great.

So, the video actually became part of my sales funnel. I'd look at a prospect's profile, see what I liked, and look for an opportunity to talk about whatever they were into, like leadership or networking.

I'd say to them, "These are some things I found about networking on LinkedIn. Can I share them with you?"

And then they'd watch the video.

I'd follow up with, "What did you think? Did you like it?" And if they told me they enjoyed it, I'd tell them that I'd love to chat with them about it, and they might book in with me for a call.

So that's one example of something that seemed kind of like a crap idea but ended up working out really well because I just did the tried and tested thing.

Your idea doesn't have to be original. It doesn't always have to be new and fresh. What people are really interested in is you. And that's what I found out with that video.

It wasn't so much a presentation of an idea as it was a presentation of who I was and what I was about. A lot of the feedback I got from it was like, "Yeah, I liked your approach to these ideas and how you connected it to me and how you want to share your ideas to help me."

Success breeds success. No matter how small the idea, or how plain or generic it sometimes seems, you won't really know what its true potential is until you put it out into the marketplace. And then, you can use the closed-loop feedback you receive to inform your next actions.

I do the same thing with my clients on LinkedIn. I say, "Okay, I've got a pretty good idea of how people react and how to hit the right points. But we're going to figure that out for you and your audience."

It's about taking in your environment and changing your approach when you need to. If we don't look at our environment consistently enough, we can move along without realizing that we're totally exposed and unsafe in our approach because we're not only offering poor value, but we could be hurting the people around us.

You have to look at what's surrounding you and act accordingly. But outside of your own cognitive biases.

That's where interactions with other people come in. It's being vulnerable enough to listen to their feedback when you're engaged.

Look Like a Branch

The stick bug, whether it feels threatened and scared or totally relaxed, will always try to mimic a branch.

If you think of them speaking, it's like they're constantly saying to themselves, "Be a branch, be a branch," at all times. They're like an artist who's completely committed to their idea.

But they will only commit to a certain extent. They'll be swaying as they're walking around, and if they see you, then they'll stop and put their arms up. They'll stay still if you touch them, but if you try to grab them, they'll bolt and run. It's like they realize, 'Oh, they made me out, I have to take off.'

They're able to blend into their surroundings really well when they're trying to avoid a threatening situation. And then, if something is aggressive with them, they just get out of there.

I think with human nature, it's like, "No, don't run away from the threat. Stick around and defend yourself."

As humans in business, even if we sense an opportunity isn't right, we might still commit to it more often than not.

On the other hand, Stick bugs really commit to what

they want to be and who they are. They really commit to being a stick.

We can learn a lot from that, in terms of commitment to your business, your work, or whatever you do. You have to think about what you want to be and commit to it.

I am almost convinced that stick bugs think they're sticks sometimes. They'll stand still looking like a stick for hours, if not days. But they've also got the muscle power to do that. They have the muscles to actually keep themselves in place.

When it comes to committing to who you want to be or who you are, or committing to how you want to show up to other people, insects, in general, provide a good example to follow.

Most insects control how much they show themselves in different areas depending on how likely they are to face a threat. They can be in potentially tricky situations but not be threatened at all due to how they commit to blending into their surroundings.

We talk about blending and mimicking and things like that quite a lot in business. I see it in the sales process. When I'm talking to people, after a while, it becomes natural for me to start mimicking what those people are doing to blend in with their ideas.

We always want to see people who are like us. Or we always want to feel like we fit into a group. So if I'm talking to somebody, and they're like me, I'll think they understand me. Part of that natural sales process is blending in with your prospects and the people you're talking to.

If you look at the stick bug species, at some point, they must have observed that sticks sway in the breeze. To avoid threats, they must have thought, 'Branches are very still, and they're long and straight, so we have to look like that.'

You can observe people in the same way to become better at sales and other interactions. I've found that learning to be like a stick bug and mimicking others helps people open up a lot more to me.

It's not that I'm necessarily being fake or anything. It's just like walking next to someone. If you decide not to walk at their pace, then you're not going to be able to keep up a conversation with them.

It's the same with business interactions. You have to mimic the process and the speed of others in order to have worthwhile dialogue.

Stick bugs observe nature and imitate it. We do the same with people—we look at them and imitate them. If you want to create true resonance with your audience, you have to do things the way they do, or look at things and think the way they do.

It's not as complicated as you think. If a stick bug can figure it out, we can figure it out too.

The stick bug observes nature. It saw what was going on, maybe over generations of genetic observation, and this has allowed it to blend into its surroundings.

'What do I struggle with the most? What do I desire to be like?' The stick bugs decided they didn't want to look like poop, though there are some caterpillars out there that look like poop, but sticks instead.

They found that they could be a part of nature without having to change their existence. Then they saw an opportunity in nature, and started resonating or echoing the same kind of behavior as sticks.

That behavior provides stick bugs with safety, and gives them more opportunities. It allows them to sit on a branch and eat to their heart's content without feeling like they have to flee whenever a bird comes along. All they have to do is stop eating and stand still.

A stick bug lets the wind blow over it and, in the same process, becomes part of its environment. In business, and life too, sometimes we have to learn to just let things blow over us.

When life blows you around, learn to roll with the wind. It's okay, it's all part of the process.

These things that are happening to you aren't really happening 'to you,' they're happening 'for you.'

I've noticed that stick bugs often won't sway like a branch getting blown around when there's no breeze. If it's windy, or you blow on them, that's when they'll begin to sway.

When you're caught in a gale, you have to learn to be like the stick bug. Take the wind, absorb it, be a part of it, and don't try to fight it.

When I kept chameleons, the only way I could get them to eat the stick bugs I fed them was to get the bugs to move. Once the chameleons recognized them moving, they would snatch them.

I once took care of my friend's chameleon for about a month while they were away. This chameleon was different from the ones I used to keep because it was always able to recognize the stick bugs, even before they moved. They had lost their charm in terms of being able to avoid being eaten by that particular lizard.

It was the same with ducks. I had so many stick bugs years ago that I took them to my friend who had ducks, and we fed the stick bugs to them.

The ducks were trying to figure out what the bugs were, and at first, I think they thought they were just grass. But ducks eat grass, so one duck went up to the stick bugs and ate one.

After that, you could see it get all excited, and it went in for some more. All the other ducks piled in then, and it just became a feast.

The learning here is that you have to pick the right camouflage depending on the predator. If you look like a piece of grass to a duck, then that's not going to do you much good.

You have to look at your environment and look at your audience. Do you want to blend in or do you want to stand out?

The best marketing is what resonates with your target market. You have to look at your audience in terms of resonance and achieve resonance with what they're looking for.

For example, my stick bugs didn't resonate with my friend's chameleon because it had already had an eye for them. The chameleon could pick them out of the environment.

But if a bird saw them in the branches of a tree, the stick bugs would be resonating with the surrounding area and be able to blend in.

Sometimes we focus too much on our message without considering whether or not it actually resonates with our audience.

We need to think, 'Is this something they're going to pick up on? Is this something that will match the same kind of frequency that they're wanting to listen to?'

Most of the time, until you put something out there and see how your audience reacts, you won't know. Then you can change your approach based on their reaction.

The stick bug, unfortunately, only gets one chance, but fortunately, we get many chances to test out new ideas and continue to grow from them.

Stick bugs give themselves chances through generations, not through individuals.

That's where their superpower is, and that's probably why they multiply so much. When you multiply yourself many times, you get a lot of opportunities to change and pass on genetic knowledge.

We can emulate generations of stick bug survival in business by looking at our audience and trying new things. We always try to write things off like 'This is our only chance,' but realistically, we have lots of chances.

We're not like a stick bug that has only one chance to resonate. We have a lot of chances to resonate with our audience and the people we interact with.

Like Johnny Appleseed

Before I went to Germany as a missionary, a lot of people asked me why I was going there. But the thing is, there are people in Germany, and where there are people, there are interactions and opportunities to learn and serve.

A lot of the work and service that we did was actually on the military base out there. A lot of the families there would have loved ones who would go away for months at a time, so we would be there to try and support them.

A lot of soldiers would also come back from Iraq with a lot of deep questions about life, so we'd get a lot of opportunities to interact with people that way.

But most of my mission was to work with German people in the German language. So I got to know a lot of locals and still find Germans really interesting because they are like the bread rolls they call "Brötchen."

In Germany, a roll is like a hard roll, but it's soft on the inside. I found Germans to be the same. They're very hard on the outside, but once you get to know them, they're very soft-hearted. You start to appreciate their culture and who they are, and what they do.

On my mission, I saw the contrast between Americans and Germans.

Americans never want to disappoint, so they overpromise and under-deliver. They say, "I can do this, I can help there, I'll be there." But then they can't follow through.

Whereas the Germans are like, "No, I can't do it, so I won't do it." And when they say they can do something, then they'll be there. It's like their standard behavior.

When I was in Germany, I was spreading service, spreading gospel, spreading love. I was also spreading a lot of stick bug eggs to try and keep my collection in check.

But for me, I guess the biggest takeaway from my time there was learning to be curious about people. If you have enough interactions, after a while, you realize you don't know much about anyone.

When you go on a mission, you think you're going to share loads of ideas with people. But when you go, you actually gain a new appreciation for the true diversity that's out there in the world. Of people and ideas. Good ideas and some not-so-good ideas.

Learning to be open to that was kind of what spurred me on when I came back from Germany years ago. I came back with a lot more curiosity than I went out with. Not only was I able to spread ideas, but I was also able to learn about other people's ideas at the same time.

Every person I interacted with had something new I could learn from. I would always think, 'Why are they the way they are? Why do they do the things they do?'

I think it's like a superpower to be curious. Not to take people at face value, but to ask them why they do things.

We are always trying to bridge the gaps in our cognitive dissonance. I went into my mission with a little bit of cognitive dissonance, saying, "We're going to share what we know. This is the truth."

There are a lot of good things that I've been able to share

with people. But at the same time, I realized that the one-on-one interactions were the coolest part. Being able to realize, 'Oh, man, that person went through so much. I don't really know how I could do what they did.' I gained empathy for people that I didn't have before.

I went out to spread ideas. And I did. But I also learned to receive other ideas from people. And that's kind of come into my business now.

I have an agenda of what I want to do when I go into an interaction with a person, but a lot of that is conditioned by what they're going through. It's really valuable to leave that flexibility and that space in the conversation to not only give an idea, but to receive an idea too.

My dad used to say, "People don't care how much you know until they know how much you care." What I have found as a missionary is that you have to learn to care for people first. Don't try to teach people until you learn to care for them. That's when the opportunities come.

It's the same in business. In my interactions online, if I can share ideas and really care about the people I interact with, then others will be open to my ideas. It's an exchange. It's not just a one-way lamplight shining into a dark place. We're actually sending and receiving light.

Engage Like a Chameleon

When I do a discovery call, it's a discovery of who the other person is.

The networking principle is that you set the stage when you go into these interactions.

I love these calls because I get to know someone new and their business and what they're trying to accomplish. And based on that, I'll know if there's something I can specifically do to help them.

I can walk a person through what that looks like, and if it's out of my realm, I'm also connected to a much larger network of other people like me that I'm happy to introduce them to if I see that there's a way that they can serve them better.

That's the stage I usually set in these calls.

With this approach, the other person usually starts to pour in, "Yeah, this is my business that I've been doing." The key is to just sit back and listen and observe, and not try to interrupt and interject.

Just let them talk.

Sometimes they'll go on for half an hour or 45 minutes. And they'll say, "Oh, I feel like I'm taking up all your time," and I'll tell them, "No, that's totally fine, that's what I'm here for, to learn about you, and I'm happy to share what I'm doing as well."

It's like this back and forth. But usually, I use the first part of a call to take the time to listen and not say anything. I almost try to mentally mute myself. I'll nod, but I don't even like to say things like "Oh yeah?" because it interrupts the other person's whole train of thought.

And if you interrupt their train of thought, they can't get out what's really on their mind.

Let others share their story, and don't interrupt them as they do so. That's the principle I always fall back on in my work.

Then, once you understand enough, you can reiterate back to them. "In your business, what's your growth like? Where do you see yourself growing? Where are you now in terms of the number of clients you have? Where do you want to be in six or twelve months? What's that going to look like? What would you be charging per client?"

And we figure out what the costs are. "What is the revenue? Okay, if you have ten customers down the road, this is what your revenue is going to look like."

That's where we start to do the dual interaction thing, where I take what they're saying, and I help paint it in color.

By the time we get to that stage, we've got a full canvas. Then I can go through what I do and see if it complements what we have been talking about.

That's kind of what creates the resonance because I already have an idea of where they want to go, and it's much easier to resonate with someone if you know where they want to go as opposed to just shooting in the dark.

I'll outline what I do, and most of the time, it's in line with what they want to do, or sometimes it's not, because maybe they're in a niche that I haven't worked in, but I have other coaches that I can refer them to.

In that case, I can enrich my network by taking on board someone's ideas, realizing that you cannot benefit them, but that someone else will.

Think of those conversations as the cross-pollination of ideas versus, "They're going to sit down and listen to what I have to say." That doesn't work anymore.

It never worked, but there was a time when people thought product sales was about telling others about your product or service. I still see this time and time again.

I, on the other hand, focus on the person. After all, it's the person who will determine if they proceed with my product or service or not.

People don't buy products, they buy you. That's the principle I try to follow, and it's worked pretty well.

Chapter 6

Bees

W orking with clients is like beekeeping.

When you start out keeping bees, you need to feed them, check on them often, and be involved.

When you begin working with clients, you need to connect with them, keep in touch, and be there to guide them.

If you work hard to do those things, then at some point, in either scenario, you'll be able to step back and recognize the fruits of your hard work.

Thinking back over the years, the first time I ever thought about keeping bees was probably when I worked at the Victoria Bug Zoo. I was around 17 or 18, and an entomologist named Carol was the owner at the time. I worked there for a season, just going in and vacuuming and cleaning early in the morning before it opened.

But it wasn't until during the COVID lockdown in 2020 that I began to realistically consider getting bees. I was thinking, 'I should probably look at more sustainable ways to take care of myself.' So, I was part of that COVID wave of people that got into beekeeping.

Later on, I came across the book 'Beekeeping for Dummies' and I thought, 'Oh, that's interesting, I should read that.' I downloaded it on Audible and listened to it. I was traveling a lot at the time, so I was able to get through it pretty quickly.

That was in December 2020. By the time I had finished it in mid-January 2021, I was thinking, 'I really like this. This could actually be the perfect thing for me right now.'

At the end of that month, I decided I was going to buy some beehives and give it a try. We had some extra money at the time, too, so I decided I would pull the trigger on it.

I started going onto YouTube to look at videos on beekeeping. YouTube has actually probably revolutionized the beekeeping world because before, the only information you could get was from people who went to bee clubs and places like that. It was a great resource to have because I didn't have to rely on people with first-hand knowledge.

I also found out that a friend who goes to the same church as me had been keeping bees for a number of years. He had three hives at the time, and I went over to his place in March of that year and helped him with his hives. I had already made up my mind about getting bees, but I was also going there to make sure that I enjoyed it before I went out and bought anything.

But it turned out that I really liked it. Being surrounded by bees flying around and not getting stung made me realize that they're actually nicer than you'd think.

I think everyone thinks they're good creatures, but there's this stigma like, "Bees are great! But don't let them near me."

Funnily enough, Brian, my friend who's been my bee-keeping mentor, is actually allergic to bee stings. He was hospitalized from a sting a couple of years ago, yet he still keeps them. He keeps himself pretty wrapped up now, but he still loves it.

I finally bought my first two hives in May 2021. I drove up to Vernon, which is about a 45-minute drive, and I got my first two nucleus hives. When you start a hive, you get these five frames in a little box with vents and stuff, so they come as nuclei.

I had decided I wanted to start beekeeping in January of that year, and I probably started buying stuff in preparation for the hives in late spring. By the end of March, I had everything done. I even built these stands for the beehives that were ant-proof. I had all this other stuff done too, and my wife said, "Man, when you get into something, you really get into it."

When the bees finally arrived later that summer, my beekeeping friend Brian came down and helped me put them in the hives. Thinking back to that first experience, I'd compare it to your wedding night, where you're thinking, 'How does this all work? What's going to happen?'

You're like a fish out of water because you're excited, but you don't know if you're doing something wrong. I was very excited, and before we knew it, the bees were in the hive.

I spent the first few weeks feeding them and getting them to grow. That year we had a record heat wave go through Kelowna; it got up to 111 degrees. I was thinking, 'Oh no, there's going to be a drought, and they're not going to get any honey,' but they actually ended up doing really well.

That first year I wasn't really expecting any honey because sometimes that's what happens when bees start out. But somehow, I ended up getting 120 pounds of honey from them.

After that, I was hooked. I was actually more into it for the bees than the honey initially, but when the honey came, I was like, 'Oh man, this is great!' I ended up selling a lot of it for 10 bucks a pound. I sold about 30 pounds, and we ate a lot ourselves. Then I ended up giving away the rest; anytime we had friends over, I was giving some away.

I called my mom yesterday when I was out on the shore surrounded by the bees, and she said, "What's that feeling you get when you're around the bees?" I said, "It's this feeling of being connected to something much bigger."

When I started beekeeping, I started noticing the flowers around me. I started seeing things like, 'Oh, there are those flowers coming up, my bees are going to enjoy them.'

When I walked around the neighborhood, I would look at people's flowers. I had never looked at flowers before, but I was saying to myself, 'Oh yeah, those are coming up, that's going to be great.' It's like I hitched my cart to the whole, big surrounding area because my bees were spreading out and going into everything. I felt a lot more connected to nature.

I've always been the type of person who looks at the weather and notices it every day. I always comment on it to my wife, and she says to me, "You know a lot more about the weather than I ever will."

But then beekeeping just kind of catalyzed that a little bit more in terms of me thinking, 'Okay, it's going to get warm next week, that's going to be great for the bees.'

I found myself looking up the types of flowers that I was seeing every day, and I became a lot more connected to what people were planting.

Before getting bees, I was the kind of person who would spray my dandelions with pesticide, but now I'm like, 'Oh, I can't do that, dandelions are actually a good thing.' I had been making sure I had the perfect green lawn, but now I'm just letting the dandelions grow a little bit more. If I want to get rid of some, I'm pulling them out manually with the little pullers. All those kinds of things started to become more important to me after I got bees because I felt that I had a stake.

Some people say that it's actually good to get stung by your bees, and one thing you notice with beekeepers is that they all have different opinions about this. I have found one consensus, and that is that you will want to get stung more than the average person, but not a ton of times.

I've decided that if I can get stung between seven and ten times a year, I'm doing pretty good. If you don't get stung enough, you can build up allergies, and the same thing can happen if you get stung too much. So if you get stung eight times in a row or something like that, things can get pretty crazy.

I just got over it, really. It still hurts the same way every time I get stung, but it doesn't last. It turns into a small mosquito bite before too long, maybe after a day, so I've built up a tolerance to being stung, which helps.

The only downside I find with beekeeping is that you can get lost in worrying about your bees because they're in their hive, and you don't really know what's going on until you're in the hive too. Even then, when you first start keeping them, and you open a hive, it's like looking into New York City, downtown Manhattan, and trying to figure out what's going on.

It's like looking at a huge canvas, but the more you look at that canvas, the more you think, 'Oh yeah, this is what's happening.' It's almost like appreciating art, and every time you pull up those frames, you're asking yourself, 'Okay, what's going on here?'

You're looking for eggs to make sure your queen bee is still alive, you're trying to find your queen, and you're making sure they have enough food, both honey and pollen. You're looking for all of that, and you're looking for mites too.

I find now, as I'm coming up to my third summer as a beekeeper, I'm learning to worry less. Last winter, I worried all winter long, 'Are my bees going to make it? I can't wait until spring to find out if they made it.' You don't really check the hive until around March, so if you don't keep a cool head, you can worry yourself out of wanting to keep bees.

In the summer, when I first got them, I was shocked when I found a bunch of dead bees outside one of the hives. I actually went out and bought one of those outdoor cameras and set it up near the entrance to the hive so I could watch it and make sure no skunks were coming in to eat the bees. It was a night vision camera, and so it's funny at night because you can actually see the dead bodies on the grass. I'd be like, 'Oh, there are so many dead bees out there.' But then I took my concern and went on YouTube and found out that it's not that bad.

Bees die all the time. They only live for 30 days, so your whole hive is basically filtered out within a month and a half to two months. It's an egg-to-cradle-to-grave kind of thing.

So I was very worried at first, especially in the winter. It would often be -10 degrees, and I'd see some bees leave the hive and fly away and never come back. I used to think, 'What's going on? Are they all committing suicide? What are they doing?'

Then I'd look into it and find out that they have purge flights where they go out and defecate because they don't defecate inside the hive.

They also do hive cleanses, where if a bee doesn't feel healthy, it will actually take off and fly away so that no one else has to drag its dead body out of the hive. When they do that, they just fly off and die somewhere. Basically, they say, "My last service to the hive is to take my dead body and put it somewhere."

Sometimes the dead ones will fall inside the hive, so the other bees will drag them up and drop them outside, and you'll have this pile of dead bees in front of your hive.

At one point, I had thought two of my four hives were probably going to be pretty weak hives. I thought I'd have to combine the two, just based on the traffic coming in and out. They're on the south side of my land, so it's a little cooler there.

But one Saturday, I went into the two hives I thought were weak, and they were just as full as the other hives. They just didn't come out as much.

So sometimes you'll think your hive isn't doing well in the winter, and you go and look and then think, 'Holy cow.' In the summer, you can get a pretty good idea of how they're doing just by looking at the traffic coming out of the hive. But in the winter, you just never really know how things are going to go.

Despite worrying about my bees early on, I think bee-keeping has done a lot more good than bad for me. Ultimately, I think feeling connected to the natural world around me has been the biggest thing to come from it. I'm connected to the flowers around me, I'm connected to what other people are planning for their fields, and I think it's cool to be connected in that way.

I think that running my business is very similar to how I tend to my beehives as a beekeeper.

In my business, I'm always thinking, 'Oh yeah, what's going on? How are people doing? Are they struggling? Are they doing well?'

There's definitely some cross-pollination in terms of how beekeeping is like managing a network.

My main outreach platform is LinkedIn, where I've got 24,000 connections. It took me six years to get to where I am, and being able to connect with that many people directly is pretty cool.

Being able to connect with people, not just in your local community, but all over the world, makes you feel like you're part of something bigger. It's not just about your own organization or your own small business, you're connecting with people in different scenarios and situations, and you get a lot of variety that way. I find the variety attractive.

When I first got into beekeeping, I was more in it for the bees than the honey. I knew I would be happy if I got into it for that reason. I decided that if I did it for the bees and not for the honey, then the honey would be a great bonus.

I think you can approach networking and networking events in a similar way. You must network with an interest in the people you'll interact with and their behaviors, their struggles, and their successes.

Placing people as my number one focus when networking and seeing anything else that may come from interactions as a bonus, has really helped change my mindset and benefited my relationships with others.

If I just focus on the money, I might get the money, but it's not going to be as rewarding as it would be if I was focused on helping the people I work with.

To grow a hive, you need to feed it. People often think of bees as wild animals, but they've been cultivated for thousands of years, probably just as long as cows have been.

Bees are basically like cattle, you have to feed them. A lot of beekeepers make the mistake of thinking, 'Oh, they'll feed themselves, I don't have to, I'll just go in and get the honey and make sure they're okay.'

You have to treat them like livestock and feed them both sugar syrup and pollen because pollen is the protein and syrup is a carbohydrate. It's especially important to do this when you first get them to ensure the colony can grow.

You also have to monitor your bees to ensure they stay healthy. I do what are called 'mite checks.' Varroa mites have been the bane of bee existence for the last 20 years. They're kind of like a tick for bees. They get on them, and then they suck their blood.

But the thing is, they do it when the bees are developing, when they're a brood in little cells. They lay their eggs on the brood, and then they hatch on the brood, so they're basically mite babies that mature inside the hive with the bee brood.

If this happens, you might have to kill off a lot of your bees, even your queen, and it can cause havoc in your hive and wreck your season.

It's also important to give your bees space, too. If the colony grows and then begins to run out of room to continue expanding the hive, the bees' natural tendency will be toward what's called 'swarming.'

The colony will create a larger-sized cell, and the queen bee will lay an egg in there. This is what's known as a queen cell, or cup, and the bees will then feed it 'queen jelly,' which is like milk that they secrete from their heads.

When any kind of developing bee gets this queen jelly, they automatically turn into a queen, which takes them from a 30-day lifespan to a 4-year lifespan.

When it's grown enough, and it's ready to pupate, the bees will seal it. Then, the existing queen and about half of the hive will fill up on honey and fly out of the hive to start a new colony somewhere else and leave the old colony for the new queen.

To prevent this, you have to keep stacking boxes on top of the hive to give the bees enough space. Otherwise, you could end up losing half your hive and a big chunk of honey, and that can set you back quite a bit.

They suggest you wear gloves when you first get into beekeeping so that you have a positive experience and getting stung doesn't ruin it for you.

But when you're wearing gloves going into a hive, you'll end up killing lots of bees because you can't feel them.

Every time I went to my hives, I would end up squishing

a load of them. Then the other bees would get mad because when you squish them, they give off an alarm pheromone, and they would sting my glove.

I remember thinking, 'Man, I'm killing so many bees every time I go in here with these gloves.' When I looked it up, I found that a lot of beekeepers didn't wear gloves when they went into hives. It seemed so counterintuitive, but I decided to try it and see how it went.

When I did this, I'd feel a bee, and it would just kind of buzz you with its wings and move out of the way. Even if I picked it up, I found that it would not be out to get me either.

Since I stopped wearing gloves, my experience has been much better. I still get stung on my fingers every now and then, but I've built up a tolerance.

I feel a lot more pleasant with the bees, and they tend to be more pleasant with me. I feel more like I'm a joint partner with them because it's like, "I'll treat you right, you treat me right."

"I might make some mistakes, but I'm going to try my best, and that's how we'll work together."

Taking the gloves off and becoming more vulnerable has made for a much better partnership with my bees.

Feed Them

You don't necessarily have to feed bees the way you feed cows, but you have to feed them to get them going.

I guess in that sense, giving them food is like creating opportunity. Dstg 8For a coach, if they don't have the opportunity to sell, then they're not really learning how to sell, and they're staying in their comfort zone.

The more people they connect with and have those conversations with, the more they learn. I compare it to the flow of the market. When a coach is just off doing their own thing, they don't get an idea of what's going on in the market for the clients that they work with.

With my outreach work through LinkedIn, I provide my clients with the opportunity to dive into that market by getting them on calls with people in their target demographic.

If they have enough of those opportunities, they'll start to get an idea of what's out there. They'll learn about some of the things that people are struggling with, and they'll learn of opportunities to help people through those things.

When they talk to enough people, they realize, 'Oh, there are some common things going on here that I think are really important.'

I think feeding my clients is almost like giving them opportunities to feel out their market and feel out their ideal customers in terms of what they're going through. Because those conversations are opportunities to take a deep dive into what's going on in so-and-so's world right now.

If someone only has a few opportunities to close a client, then that's all they'll be thinking about. But if you give them opportunities to actually engage prospects, then it changes their mindset a little bit more.

If there's enough feed or enough opportunities out there, they won't have to worry about the immediate side of things. They can actually start to tap into the market and gain insights that can actually help them close customers.

I think the insight gained is probably the biggest part of it. You need to understand a person before you can get to selling to them. I think creating opportunities for people is what feeds them enough to get the confidence to ask the right questions and really engage their prospects to the point of turning them into clients.

I usually get the people I work with to the point where they get a client. Once they get the client, my role is to keep pushing them like, "Okay, were you able to get a referral? Were you able to get a testimonial from them? That would be really cool."

A lot of my focus is also on that first conversation they have with someone, and I'll try to help my clients learn from those experiences.

People will often talk about how they want to grow and do all these other things, but often they'll have one big issue that's stopping their progress. I'll ask my clients, "What was the problem that they actually turned around and said, 'I want to talk to you about this.' Did you find out what that deep issue was?"

If you can get an understanding of what that real problem is and what it's costing someone, then you've got something to talk about. Whereas, if a person is saying, "Yeah, I want to grow, and I want a coach to kind of push me along," you're not really getting enough information from them to really sell yourself to them.

They have to be guided toward the point where they're saying, "If I don't continue the status quo of what I'm doing here, I'm going to lose X amount of growth, or I'm going to lose X amount of people."

When one of my clients helps that become clear in a prospect's mind, then all of a sudden, they are on the path to growth.

Monitor Them

From my observations, many coaches sell coaching assignments that they usually charge upfront for. And then they've got all these clients who paid them, but they still have to deliver the goods in terms of service.

Sometimes they'll sit there for a while and not go about delivering. They'll have all these accounts they've received payment from, but they haven't delivered on the service promised yet.

It can build up to where they might have like 20 clients, and maybe the coach feels they only have the time to work with half of those people.

But that's not very good practice for their business.

I think it's very important to learn how to show up for your clients.

Beehives are nice in that you don't necessarily have to check in on them that often, but when you're starting out, especially in the beginning, you must check in on them every three weeks to see what's going on and how their growth is developing.

As they start to mature into a full hive, then you're really just checking to make sure they have enough space to grow in the summertime, so they don't swarm out on you.

It's the same with clients, where in the beginning, you need to touch base and connect with them often because they're still growing into the person they want to become.

A good way to do that is to set the stage at the beginning. Coaches are usually pretty good at this, like asking how often a client wants to meet. A lot of coaches will say they want to meet their client once a week to start with, and then they'll work towards meeting every two weeks.

They often don't go beyond two weeks, I find, because it's important to be a part of a client's growth cycle. Especially in the beginning, the more frequently they meet with someone, the better, but after that, coaches tend to split into two different groups.

You have the fixer coaches, who are the ones that just want to get in there and fix their clients' situation and get them independent as quickly as possible because that's going to make for a really good referral down the road.

There are others that want to help their clients get to where they want to go, but they want to continue to help them along the way and get them not just to 'goal A,' but to 'goal B' and beyond.

Both approaches can work well. I tend to work more with the fixer coaches because they go and fix people's situation as quickly as possible. That means they've got to have clients coming in all the time, and that's where I help them out a lot.

Long-term coaches usually don't need that many clients. I usually produce about two to three clients a month for many of the coaches I work with, but if you're a long-term coach, you might need one client every couple of months.

Usually, coaches like that tend to charge more, so if I produce one client for them every couple of months, it could pay them maybe three grand a month. That type of revenue can make for a really good relationship with this type of coach, too.

With my business, especially in the beginning, I make myself available to my clients. I think that's really vital. I'm available as often as they need me, and early on, we'll probably be touching base at least once a week.

If something comes up, and they want to chat, I'm more than happy to do that. I keep my client base at a level where I can be available at the drop of a hat on the day that they need me. I don't book my days solid with stuff, I keep some gaps in there so that when clients come to me with questions, we can hop on a call right away.

I think it's important to never overbook yourself so much that you're not available to your clients when they need you. That helps alleviate a lot of fear from them at the beginning of your relationship in terms of them wondering, 'Is this person only going to be available to me every couple of weeks? What if I have a question or a concern that comes up?'

After a while, you kind of establish that groove with your client. But in the beginning, you can say, "Let's meet at least once a week, or as often as you need me available." That's the approach I take with my practice. Some coaches will package appointments and that works too, because their client will pay for so many appointments, and they can have them as often as they want.

There's almost a sweet spot for how many clients you want to have. Usually, having more than 10 clients will make it difficult for you to be available for them all in terms of one-on-one coaching.

Make sure you have the availability to really be there to help your clients.

Give Them Space to Grow

Just like giving a bee colony space to expand, you need to give clients opportunities to grow.

What that looks like, in my business, is seeing how we can get a coach to the point where they're getting more and more content out for their prospects.

As they're diving into the marketplace, I'm there to help them identify opportunities through our conversations.

After they've been on some calls with potential clients, I might say, "Okay, you mentioned a couple of people who had the same problem, didn't you? If you see that some people have the same problem, maybe we should talk about that in our prospecting?"

"If that's a common problem in this industry right now, maybe we should share that insight with your network and see how they respond?"

If you're looking for common problems that have common solutions, then you'll have an evergreen approach for when you reach out to potential clients.

If a coach sees some common threads across multiple conversations, that's gold, because it'll help them recognize problems that they can provide solutions to.

Then they can put together some content for their network, which is something that not many coaches do. Usually, that content might take the form of a video, which can be really effective. But there's a self-image part that they have to go through for that.

'Am I comfortable on camera? Do I feel comfortable putting my picture up here? I don't really feel like I'm attractive in terms of how I look.'

I talk through those challenges with a lot of clients, because coaches are often very 'heads down.' They think, 'I'm here to fix the problem, but I'm not really here to broadcast myself." It's a little bit of a sticking point for them sometimes.

If it's a big sticking point for a coach, we can work from different angles. We can say, "Let's find another way to grow here; maybe we just stick to email, or maybe we stick to messaging. Are there things you can share in terms of video screen sharing, maybe where it doesn't have your image?"

We are now in an age where people feel they really need to see someone to consider working with them. So I'll often work with coaches to help them realize that people are not interested in how they look, but rather how much they care, how much they know, and how much they can help them.

A coach's appearance is the last thing on most prospects' minds. If you can just focus on your knowledge and what you're sharing, your looks don't really matter. Make sure you have a good background, make sure you look professional, but beyond that, nothing else really matters.

When I go into relationships with clients, trust is, in essence, space. They trust me enough to give me the space to do what I need to do, and I trust them enough to give them the space to do what they need to do.

Once I've got them to a point where they are doing sales calls and figuring out the issues, and selling their service, I give them that space. We check in afterward, but I don't say, "You have to record your calls, let me listen to your calls, and then we'll talk about it."

If they're willing to do that, great, but it's more like, "Okay, walk me through how it went." It's not like it's a formalized debrief of their call. I'll ask them how it went, and we'll see what they learned from it.

It's about giving them the space to be a professional coach and then being there for them enough to help them with their growth in sales and other aspects of their business. I also want to be the person that they can trust enough to take care of their entire outreach and inbox. They can think, 'I don't have to check my inbox and respond to these people, he's on it.'

If I get a coach that checks their inbox, I'll make sure that there's nothing missing in terms of trust and see if I can grow off of that.

Extract the Honey

The 'Sword Of Truth' book series talks about 'journey before destination.' I think you can adopt a similar mindset when it comes to extracting the honey from a beehive.

It's about learning to enjoy and appreciate the journey and not necessarily the destination because then you won't miss out on all the stuff in between. If honey is the only thing you're excited about with beekeeping, then you're only excited about August every year and the rest of the time, it's just work.

If you're interested in the actual bees and their behavior and the changes and all the things that are going on, then you'll be excited all year round. That's my thought process.

I've seen so many people lose opportunities along the way because they are so focused on the outcome that they want.

I think the problems start when someone loses interest in their work. They lose focus on the journey and focus so much on themselves that they forget why they started out.

My business of getting new clients for coaches was really about feeding my desire to help people and then being curious enough about them to dig deeper. That's why I work with coaches, because they help people, and they're curious by nature. But that curiosity can sometimes get lost when they focus on the desired results or the honey.

When beginning to work together, a lot of coaches will say to me, "I want to grow, I want to get more clients, I want to make more money."

So what I do is try to get them to rediscover their curiosity. I'll do this by being curious myself and asking them detailed questions to help them refind themselves.

"Tell me how you're doing it? Why do you do it that way? Why do you like being a fixer coach? How does that build you up?"

It's just asking those questions to get them to really think deeper in terms of the surface level of what they do and why.

It starts to build that vision and that trust a bit more, and they can start to enjoy their work again. If they're excited about what they do every day, then the honey will come automatically.

Take the Gloves Off

Vulnerability is funny. Coaches are generally good at it, but people always have vulnerabilities that they try to shield.

I found out that one of the coaches I work with is a drummer. He has this whole mentality of 'I'm here to make you sound good and create this resonance in your life and get the ideal frequency of how you want to live and make you look good.'

It's funny because it scared him to embody that initially. He loved it, but it scared the hell out of him to share that part of himself with people. He didn't know if people would get the wrong impression if they saw him as a drummer; there's a certain vulnerability in that. I'm learning that myself just by going through this book. At the start of this process, I didn't really want to talk about mistakes I made because I didn't think people would be interested in that.

When it comes to coaches, there's vulnerability in terms of them thinking, 'I don't want to show my face in front of a bunch of people online.'

They might worry that somebody will say something if they put themselves out there, and it will sting them. But that's okay because it's going to get to the right people too, and obviously, that person is not the right person.

That vulnerability comes through direct outreach all the time. When you're reaching out to hundreds of people, you're going to get one or two that are on a bad day, and they're going to give you the "What for." At first, you're going to freak out and think, 'Oh no, we have to change our approach!'

I fall into this all the time too. I had one person who booked with me, and I sent him some video testimonials before the booking, and he kind of interpreted it as me trying to be lazy and do all this automation, so I wouldn't have to do as much work on the call. He canceled the call, and I was like, 'Crap, do I need to do things differently?'

But I realized he was the first person, out of several hundreds, that had gone through the same sort of approach, so I thought to myself, 'Maybe I'm going to wait and see.'

You have to take the gloves off and expose yourself to people's comments and moods at the moment. Through that process, you will start to gain an understanding of a lot more people, and you'll be able to connect with a lot more people.

You also build up a tolerance over time. Yes, things are always going to hurt the same at first, but you'll get over it a lot faster. You have to expose yourself to what people think in order to get through it, because then you'll start looking forward to the people who are right for you. If you're not getting stung enough, you're not really stretching yourself enough.

We often try to restrict the people in our social groups to those we are comfortable with. We want to have people over that we know we're going to like, or we want to associate with people that we know we like.

But the best relationships I've had in my life are often with people who were not the typical people I thought I'd like to be around. It takes a certain amount of vulnerability to be able to connect with and find those people.

I've found that you can connect people much more in terms of their pain, their struggles, and what they're going through. We often try to avoid that socially. We try to focus on the good things that are going on in someone's life, and that's what we usually talk about.

If you can start to share more of the things that aren't going well in your life like, "Oh, I tried this, and it totally didn't work," and you can be okay with that, people will start to see that you're okay with making mistakes.

I see that with my parents. They were really good examples of that growing up; we started going to a new church when we were younger, and they were learning along with us, and their whole mantra was, "You make parents out of us, we don't have all the answers." Their parenting style, whenever it came to making moral decisions, was to say, "I don't feel like it's the greatest idea because of this and this, but we'll leave it up to you to decide." Them giving me that space to make my own decisions helped to create a much deeper relationship between us.

I think it's the same with business relationships or personal relationships. Giving people the freedom to make their decisions helps them with a variety of different things, all the while exposing yourself to them making a decision that you might not agree with.

It's the same with bees, they might sting me, and they probably have a good reason for that, but I trust that overall it's going to be okay. I give them the benefit of the doubt. I think that's the biggest part of any relationship, to believe that they're trying their best, and they're only stinging you because they felt justified at the time. It's thinking, 'They probably were justified, but I'm going to get over it and try to find common ground again.'

The first time I took my gloves off and reached into the beehive, I kind of had to say, "Let's see how this goes." I get that with clients too. "Let's try this and see how it goes." Then, once you've gone through the experience, together you can open it up and see what actually happened there.

After observing how many bees I was squishing when going into my hives, I thought, 'Oh, maybe I should take my gloves off because I'm hurting more than I'm helping here.'

With that approach, I was essentially thinking, 'Can I help more if I become more vulnerable? If I become more vulnerable, what are some of the possible outcomes?' It was about going in with curiosity to see what happened.

It's the same with anything uncomfortable, like turning the shower to cold at the end of your shower. It's never pleasant, but once you do it, you realize there's something liberating about it. Any kind of growth always takes a bit of pain, but then it's often liberating right after.

It's about saying, "Okay, I didn't get a good result there. Let's maybe try it one or two more times." Like with my bees for instance, if I get stung three times, then I'll put my gloves back on for a bit. I need to absorb the venom to build up a tolerance, but I don't want to overwhelm myself with it.

I know that if I get stung a couple of times, I can always put my gloves back on to make sure I have a pleasant experience overall.

It's not like you have to expose yourself to thousands of stings. You're not taking your gloves off permanently, you're taking them off long enough to gain some experience and get stung a couple of times.

What is the benefit of cultivating clients this way? I would say it leads to much longer-lasting and deeper relationships because you're covering ground together.

You're going on this journey with them, and you're also being vulnerable in your approach and saying, "Okay, I tried this, it didn't work, but here's what we're going to do to overcome this." Being able to admit that as a coach or any kind of professional is really important.

Admit your failures, but also expand on what you're going to do to overcome those failures. We always like to think that things are perfect, but they're not. There are always nuances that we don't expect. But as long as I'm with someone who's willing to be innovative and vulnerable, I think that's really important. If a person is not vulnerable, then I don't want to be alongside them in a gunfight. I think by being vulnerable, you're showing me that you're comfortable being uncomfortable, so if we get into challenging situations, you've got my back.

If you take that approach with people, you'll have clients who know you have their back. You'll have relationships that you'll be able to cultivate in such a way that when a person hires you as a coach or when a person allows you to serve them, they'll allow you to serve them because they trust you.

You'll be able to build trust with clients that you wouldn't normally be able to build trust with. They see that there's somebody there for them that's got their back, and they can trust your process, and they can relate to your process because sometimes that's a challenge as a coach.

The more you understand your prospects and what they're going through in the market that they're in, the deeper your ability will be to connect with that and resonate with them. It's important that you are able to resonate with your clients, not just tell them what to do. That only comes through being exposed to the market-place that they're in on a consistent basis.

You're going to make mistakes. I lost my first 2 hives in my first year of beekeeping. I could have thrown in the towel and said, "Oh man, it's going to cost so much more to get results again." But I didn't, I found a way to make it work, and now things are going great.

Get comfortable taking the gloves off, and if you're not comfortable yet, just try it a few times. It will help you understand your network and understand your clients. Through that understanding, you'll be able to connect on a deeper level than you ever have before.

Chapter 7

People

I 've spent most of this book talking about all kinds of animals ... but not people. So, fellow humans, now let's talk about you.

The first people we encounter in our lives here on earth are the members of our family.

As a child, I spent a lot of time with my family. If I wasn't playing with bugs, I was with them.

My mom came from a family of six kids, so I had lots of cousins. We often got together with them while I was growing up, so interacting with my close and extended family was my first exposure to people outside my immediate family.

I ended up learning that families were different. As you grow up, you tend to feel that your family is the smartest and the best and that other families are all kind of crazy. You grow up with that paradigm, and then you realize the truth.

It's funny, I'm still discovering things. I look at my cousin Matt's family and how they pulled together through his cancer. His mom passed away a year ago from a heart attack, and I saw how they pulled together without her, even though she had been the glue in their family.

Then Matt passed away, and it seems to have strengthened them even more. Seeing families pull together like that makes you realize that those initial observations you made about other families as a child were not the most correct.

As I got older, I had to decide who I wanted to spend my time with and who I wanted to be around in terms of friends and family. In some ways, that was chosen for me. Growing up, I didn't drink and didn't smoke, both religiously and also kind of naturally.

When I was in high school, it quickly became apparent in grade 9 or 10 that I wasn't really the type of person other kids would want to invite out to parties, even though I wanted to go. It's funny because I remember coming home on the bus one day, and my friends were all talking about the party they were going to, and I said, "Oh, that'd be fun. Do you need a designated driver?"

One friend replied, "Tyson, no, you wouldn't want to go, this isn't your scene." I felt like they were really saying, "No, no, no, we don't want you to come." I remember coming home in tears and talking to my mom and saying, "Who am I going to hang out with?"

Looking back to that pivotal moment, I'm so grateful

for that friend who told me that the party wasn't my scene. I'm grateful for the inspiration that he had, even if it was self-serving, because what ended up happening at that point was that my siblings stepped in.

My sister is ten years older than me, so she was in her early 20s, but still living at home. She would always include me in events she planned with her friends. She had a lot of friends through church, and when they went up to Vernon to go to a hot tub party, she'd bring me along.

In ninth and tenth grade, it was really great to have her. It wasn't like I went up with her all the time, but just enough to think, 'You know, I am kind of cool.' That's all you really need to think as a kid.

My brother did this too. He's seven years older than me, and he always said that he wanted to live his life vicariously through me.

Having my siblings there for me was really helpful during that time in high school. They showed me the first fundamentals of caring for other people around you. They taught me how important it was to make others feel cool and special.

Even though the friends I had grown up with through elementary school felt that I wasn't cool anymore once we got to high school, my siblings kind of poured into me that way.

I'm so glad that I had them because if I didn't have them, I think I would have probably come out of my youth with a far different view of myself and who I was. They did a good job of making me feel cool, even when maybe I wasn't cool whatsoever.

My first experience of really dealing with people outside of my family members was when I went to go and serve for my church in Germany. The way it's done is that you go out for two years, and you don't go home at all. We'd only call home at Christmas and on Mother's Day.

I was there from 2004 to 2006, and that time was probably the most focused I've ever been, and probably will ever be, on one thing.

Before heading away, we underwent training for two months. We spent about three-quarters of each day doing language training, and then the remainder learning about the Bible.

We learned how to teach, and teach concepts in a different language. Then they flew us off to Germany, and I began the mission.

Acquiring the ability to listen was of huge importance over there. I learned to stop and just listen to people. And my desire to listen to people grew.

It wasn't necessarily as much about me going out and telling people what to do, but learning to listen to them, and through that listening, helping to comfort them.

I realized that it only takes a fraction of words to comfort someone. It is about being there, listening, appreciating, and following their story and what they have to say.

I learned to slow down enough to listen, and I think that has translated into my business today.

I also learned that no matter who a person is, they've always got a really profound story and experience. In business, you can't go into a meeting with someone and expect to know what they're going through.

In Germany, I was exposed to all sorts of things. One of the guys in my area had AIDS that he got from Prince back in the 1980s. He was one of the longest-lived people in that part of Germany with AIDS.

He was one of the members of our ward, and he'd call all the time and chat with us because he was still suffering through it. The array of different experiences I was exposed to helped me to understand that you can't judge anyone for their past, and that everyone's their own unique person.

This experience taught me to go into business meetings with a more open mind and to not have a preconceived perception of what I think someone is going to teach me or what they're going to say.

That approach has helped me a lot in my business, because I'm seeing new things every day. I can never go into a meeting and expect it to have a certain outcome. That mindset of going into things with an open mind has changed the way I start relationships in business.

I learned that when you want an experience with someone to turn out a certain way, or you want to be able to have a certain influence, but you don't know how to get to that point with people, you have to trust that someone's got you along the way.

I saw that a lot on my mission. It's when things are beyond your line of sight, and you can see where you want to be, but everything in between where you are, and there is a cloud of doubt and fear.

'I have the tool set I have, and whatever I'm missing is going to be taught to me through my experiences.' That kind of visionary mindset started to come out early on when I was on my mission.

I'm seeing that more as an entrepreneur. Often, there's a lot of fog and doubt when it comes to whatever I'm doing. I can paint the picture of where my business is going to end up, but there's a lot to figure out on the fly as we go. I learned to get comfortable with that on my mission.

On my mission, I would sometimes feel like I had been cast out in this strange area, and I didn't know what I was going to make of it. I was always hoping that I was going to have a positive impact and that my companion, who was more experienced than I, was not going to freak out or go home and all these other things.

So, eventually, I learned to work through doubt and fear.

I think what I learned is that whether it's God, or whatever you call it, there's someone watching out for us. It's about having a mindset that involves thinking, 'It's going to be okay.'

It's not necessarily that someone's watching out for me, so I can just relax. It's that someone's watching out for me, and they're going to help me to take my actions and make them work for my good.

That belief has kind of stuck with me. 'I'm going to do my best, and it's going to work out in the end.' I learned to trust that things will work together for my good.

I think maintaining relationships with faith is so important. It's about having faith in each other and faith in the process.

As we interact with different people in our lives, we might start to feel a resonance with certain people, and faith can only be born from that kind of feeling.

I see this in all my business interactions. The clients that have stuck with me for a while say, "I really like the fact that you're being genuine in your approach with people." I guess it's that there's not a sense of insecurity there.

If you can learn to go into relationships with a faith that rules out the insecurity that we often have, you can lay the foundation to building really solid relationships.

People talk about faith as more of a religious thing, but it's not. Faith is in everything that we do. All of our interactions are built on it.

I've learned to have faith in myself, but also have faith in being able to build with others. It's not about shouldering the whole burden of success and taking all the

197

joy of success, but learning to shoulder that burden and work together with others to achieve your goals.

I'm not celebrating myself, I'm celebrating with others, and I'm not achieving myself, I'm achieving with them. It's really important to take that mindset through the work that we do.

Find Your Mentor

I wasn't always the best listener. I think good listening comes through training or God-given talent, and I was probably not the best-trained listener for quite a good part of my life. That was until Dani Johnson came back in 2013.

My wife's mom told her about Johnson being a really good, effective salesperson and a mentor to follow. My wife read her book and said, "Tyson, you should really read this."

It was Johnson's first book, *Spirit Driven Success*. The idea behind it was that we've already got the tools to have effective sales conversations, but we have bad habits that we've developed in our nature and our behavior. So once we correct those habits, we can all be good salespeople.

I was in banking at the time, and I was managing a bank branch in a small town. We had just had our first two kids, and then we had a newborn. At that point, I remember being at a stage where we were running pretty tight.

I was the sole breadwinner, and my wife was at home, and we had racked up some debt. The biggest thing with Dani Johnson is that she teaches people how to get out of debt, and so that drew me into her work.

My wife liked her whole sales thing, and I really liked the whole debt thing of figuring out where the fat is in your budget and cutting it off.

We found out that Johnson was doing live events, and there was one going ahead down in Austin, Texas. We fronted the money on our credit card and went down to see it. It was our first leap of faith in ourselves, like 'Let's see what we can learn.'

The biggest thing we came back from that event with was that we were making enough money but spending too much, so we needed to cut back on our spending. The first thing we did was cancel our cell phone plans.

I decided, 'I work at the bank, I don't need a cell phone.' Johnson kind of brain-ninja'd us in a way. "You don't need a phone, people need phones for emergencies, everyone's got a phone, so you can just ask them for their phones."

We then canceled our TV and any kind of subscription stuff we didn't need. We cut and tied back our spending to the point where the rest of my family was noticing. They said, "You've really gone crazy here."

But we started to save money; we ended up getting a consolidation loan that my grandparents cosigned on, and that was the first step we took in really taking control of our finances.

Find your bait and let it pull you in. My bait was finances at the time, it wasn't listening to people. The biggest thing is learning to follow the things that are most important to you. I was baited in with 'I need to get out of debt,' but what I came out with was so much more.

If your biggest thing is "I would like to learn how to talk to people or how to listen to people," that's great, and important. To help you get there, I would always recommend you find a mentor.

Dani was the first mentor I ever paid in my life. Before that, I used to think, 'You don't pay mentors, they just take your money, and you don't really get much out of it.'

We paid her a lot of money too. We went to 8 or 9 of her events all over the US, which was kind of cool because I got to see cities I'd never been to, like New York and all these other great places.

We probably spent about 30–40 grand in about 4 years, but that started our process of learning to invest in ourselves. Johnson was the first person to teach me to do that.

At first, I thought, 'Of course she's telling me to invest in myself, because there are people at the back of this room who are ready to take my credit card.' That was my hang-up at the beginning.

But then we paid all that, we went back home, and we saved so much more money and got ourselves into a much better position. Every time we'd go to an event and come back home, we'd end up better off.

During that time, I also learned to join and be surrounded by communities of like-minded thinkers. The fact that everyone that went to these live events was so positive really appealed to me.

Everyone there was working towards the same goals. It became so much easier to accomplish things once we were surrounded by like-minded thinkers, or at least people striving for the same goals.

I came away from those events with a community and an understanding that if I paid money to have mentors teach me how to better myself, I ended up making more money in the long run. And those two things are kind of what fueled me to find mentors in the future.

Later on came Sam Ovens, and he had this course that was priced at $2,000. But we did it. Then another mentor I found wanted to charge me $6,000 to show me how to do LinkedIn, and I said, "Sure, no problem."

Going down this road together with my wife was a big part of it. I realized how important it is to walk with people who are important to you. Learning to pay to invest in myself and then learning to surround myself with communities is what came out of my mentorship journey.

Over the years, I've realized that the top-performing people in the world, like CEOs and billionaires, all choose to invest in finding mentors and communities too.

I believe that those two things are the secret to success in many ways.

Listen

If you want to comfort someone, you need to listen to them with true, genuine curiosity and interest. That interest comes through personal development and getting outside your own head.

When you take the time to listen, then the right words of comfort will come to your mind. You can't really create those words of comfort out of thin air. They just don't come.

But when you're listening to someone, and you're empathizing with their situation or empathizing with their plans or goals, then you can comfort them automatically because your empathy draws it out.

When you go through sales calls, do not interrupt someone in their thoughts, let them talk and leave pauses for them to think. Even leave awkward pauses, sometimes for up to a minute.

I learned to get comfortable with minute-long pauses while talking to people, and that helped me tremendously to be able to slow down enough to really listen.

Through that listening, you'll start to get pulled towards

people's goals and plans. Allowing someone the space to share those things can work like magic when you're trying to get to know someone.

I would say that at least 75% to 85% of my business success has been from listening, and listening is as easy as not talking.

We always come to that stage in a conversation where we feel like we need to offer someone else advice, saying, "Oh, I have this cool idea." I still get caught in this when I get excited about something, and I have to slow myself down.

It's like, 'I'm getting excited about the direction that I could possibly take this conversation in, but no, let's hold back. Let's just stop thinking in my head and let it go blank and listen to what the person's saying.'

That thought process has been the biggest part of my success in business.

Whenever I feel overwhelmed by feeling like I need to come up with a solution on calls with my clients, I say to myself, 'I just need to sit back and listen more,' or 'Let's ask some more questions here.'

Back in December, things were kind of slowing down a bit with one of my clients, and she said, "I may need to pause our work together through Christmas."

After Christmas, she said, "I decided to do Tony Robbins. I want to figure out what my brand is. I think we need to change our approach a bit in terms of how I represent myself with these conversations, so when we pick it up again, we're really strong going into it."

She's already got a great presence, we built up a really good audience, and she's sitting at 23,000 connections on LinkedIn. What came out of this is that all these people are starting to come back to her now.

This even includes some people we reached out to two years ago. We sent one message to them on LinkedIn, and then they're all of a sudden responding back two years later!

Maybe people just don't check their LinkedIn very often, but now they're saying, "Yeah, I want to have a meeting." She ended up getting 5 new clients last month, and I think two or three of those were courtesy of the campaign that we have been running for the last 2 months.

She already had the brand, and I think people see her as a certain person beyond what she sees herself as sometimes. We put together a plan for that, and I'm so glad we did because I was thinking of bringing on a partner, but then we ended up going in a different direction.

The client said, "I've got to figure out what I want, and Tyson, you've got to figure out what you can do to help get me there." So then we just came away with, "Okay, this is what we're going to do."

Most people think, 'I'm going to flip some options up to my client, and then they can tell me which ones they like.' But they should instead be taking an approach where they look at the big picture; examining what their client wants to accomplish and then breaking down the fine details of that with them.

"Your ideal client is this and this. You want to be able to generate how many clients?"

Then, with those factors, you can start to present solutions based on what they're looking for, rather than just trying to give them swatches to pick from.

Open Mind

I try to avoid going too deep into people's LinkedIn profiles before jumping on a call with them. The only thing I'll look at is their job title and whether or not they are in the same industry as me. I'll look at where they live too, because I'm always curious about that.

When someone starts to talk about a place I'm not familiar with, I'll always say, "Show me where it is on a map."

If someone has detailed where they live on their LinkedIn profile, I'll look it up. 'Where do they live? Okay, they're in this city. Is that on the ocean? Have I been there before? Would I want to go there one day?'

I'll look at some of their posts, just to see if they're active, and just to get an idea of how they think. I might look at how long they've been in the coaching business too. That helps me to understand if they are new to the space or experienced. It helps me decide what type of approach I will take with them, and what kinds of questions I'll ask them.

But I try not to go too deep into it all because I don't want to feel like I know anything about them as a person yet. I just want to answer questions about them in terms of their history and where they live, just the peripheral things.

In terms of questions about their business, I'll look at their profile enough so that if they ask if I've looked at their profile, I can say, "Yeah, I have looked at it."

But I don't want to look at it so much that I get to a point where I feel like I understand who they are before I even talk to them. I want to understand a bit about their circumstances, but I don't want to understand who they are until they have the chance to actually tell me themselves.

This helps in that first initial conversation I have with someone to really allow my curiosity to flow. If I satisfy it before I even hop on a first call, then it makes it harder to allow my curiosity to run rampant.

The call itself is really where I want my curiosity to be unleashed because the person is right there, and I can ask them any question that comes to mind.

People need to tell their story first. If you don't give them that chance, then you won't understand them, and the biggest part of a relationship starts with understanding and being able to appreciate who someone is.

When I begin to talk to someone new on LinkedIn, I always try to suspend my curiosity, so I can save it for when we're on a call.

Curiosity is kind of your secret weapon in terms of being able to connect with people. It's curious people that actually do the best work in any business, really. Whether it's finance or coaching or whatever it is, curiosity is crucial.

In business, I think it's important that you don't satisfy your curiosity too early. You need to treat your curiosity like a dessert, don't eat it up all at once.

All humans are curious by nature, but often we're only curious to the point where we feel like we've figured out the answer to our problem and the moment we think we've figured out that answer, we stop looking.

That's the trap that we all fall into. If we get to a point where we feel satisfied enough with the answer, then we stop looking, and we stop digging. We stop asking.

The business principle here is to know yourself enough to know when you feel like your curiosity is saturated. Once you understand that, you can coax yourself along to stay curious.

When people aren't curious, it's because they've satisfied their curiosity too early, or they've allowed themselves to be satisfied too early.

In my line of work, you can draw that out in a number of different ways. My strategy is to wait until I'm in front of a person, either in a face-to-face interaction, or on the phone.

Even with the podcasts that I've done over the years, I try to save my curiosity about the host for the meeting. You want to know enough about them to say, "This would be an interesting conversation," but then save the interesting conversation for when you're talking to them in person.

It's the same thing as a doctor prescribing medication to you. If your doctor comes into an appointment with a closed mind, they're going to misdiagnose you and misprescribe you, right?

If you don't go into business conversations with an open mind, your solution might not be the best solution for the other person. Unless you really listen to their problem, you won't be able to prescribe the right solution.

Entering a meeting with an open mind means letting someone tell you what they want and need. Then, if you feel they are a fit for what you do, it will help you to position your product or service in relation to what they want and need. If it's not a fit, that's fine too, at least now you understand enough to be able to refer them to someone in your network.

Hopefully, you've got a network built up where you can do that, and if you don't, then start building that network now. That will give you the ability to refer your clients to who they need so that everyone that comes to you will always get a solution.

It may not come from you directly, but it will come through you. Being able to come at life as that sort of 'connector' changes the whole dialogue.

Sometimes you'll go into conversations thinking, 'I don't think I'm going to help this person.' But if you have a network, it's like, 'No, I'm going to be able to help this person, whether it comes directly from me or through referring them to someone else.'

That mindset will change your whole footing in conversations with potential clients and your positioning with them.

Work Through Doubt and Fear

When I was in banking, I lived in a very comfortable sort of world. In that world, you know what you're going to make every year, and you always have a job for the most part, as long as you don't do something stupid.

I went from that position of being totally comfortable to starting my own business and relying on my wits and my intellect and leaving everything else up to divine intervention. I went from comfort to this place of total discomfort and doubt.

I remember during the months when I was first starting out, I was thinking, 'If I lose a client, will I be able to pay my mortgage next month?' I had those types of fears.

It sometimes pushed me beyond my capacity to really find the answers and solutions when challenges arose. And that's something that I was missing before when I was in banking, because I hadn't needed to do that.

I was listening to a podcast yesterday, and this billionaire was talking about "The tractor beam of entrepreneurship." That phrase rang true with me when I think of how I started my business.

You almost have to be a bit of a gambler to be an entrepreneur. It pulls you in because of the fear and the risk. But you also realize that you start to rely on things outside of yourself as an entrepreneur, because you have control over a finite amount of your business.

The rest is up to your team and up to the clients that you take on to work with. It can be left to economic factors, too, and things like that become more of a thing for you because you don't have the protection of being a corporation.

It's so funny how entrepreneurship pulls you into all of that. I often think, 'Why did I get into this more uncomfortable situation where I have to wake up so early and study and do all these things?'

The answer is, I wanted to have freedom. I wanted to have the ability to create my life and not have it created for me.

The best way to start a business or do whatever you want is the way that you know how, with what you've got. And the more you're open to learning more, the better your process becomes. There's no real perfect way of doing it, so that's the best alternative.

People always think that when you start a business, it has to be done in a certain way. When I first started, we had just bought a house, and we moved into the basement suite.

We didn't have any extra space in our room. It was a two-bedroom basement suite, one room for the kids, one for us, and I didn't have a room for my office. I was tired of working on the coffee table, like the classic startup, so I built my own kind of standing desk.

It almost looked like a spine because it was a structure that had all these little slots in it. I made two boards that fit into the slots, one for my laptop and one for my keyboard, so that it was kind of ergonomic.

I put it in my laundry room, which wasn't very big. It was this long alcove, and then it had my desk. That was my first office, this totally uncomfortable spot.

The mentor Sam Ovens actually commented on it in one of his live courses. He said, "It's funny, we have this thing on Facebook where people are sharing the offices that they had, and I saw this guy that had this office in a laundry room. He had this little standing desk, and it looked so uncomfortable!"

And the principle he was trying to teach at the time was, "Don't make an office in a place where you don't want to be because you won't get any work done there." But it's funny because I look back to when that picture was taken, it was actually just before I had my biggest month yet in terms of revenue–I made 10 grand.

The best way to do business is the best way you know how, and the more you can learn, the better. Don't be totally reliant on other people's opinions, do the best you can with what you have. That's how I started.

I think any entrepreneur, whether they're in North America, Africa, or Asia, will start with something basic and simple that they know they have. They then go out and find people to add to that.

Don't think that you have to come up with a perfect process from the beginning. Do the best that you can, and then start to go out and bring in ideas, and those ideas will either work or they won't work.

Now, I look back to that picture of me in my laundry room office, and I think that time is a pretty cool part of my development. Humble beginnings are okay.

Act In Faith

A previous client's first step of faith with me gave me faith in myself.

I've been running campaigns since January 2020 with this client, whom I've had for three years now. We started working together just before all the crazy COVID stuff, but we were still able to generate business for her throughout that time.

Very early on, I remember her saying, "Tyson, I really get a good feeling about you. I'm the type of person who is going to take care of you if you take care of me, and this is going to be great."

That was our first step together. It always resonated with me throughout our whole relationship, because she actually did that. There were months when things were slower or when I had a new approach that I wanted to bring in, and she'd always say "I trust you Tyson, you'll figure this out." And we figured it out, it always worked out.

You kind of have to let go. I remember this girl I dated once said, "You know, love is like a butterfly, if you sit there, it might land on you. But if you chase it, it'll fly away."

It's kind of like that with any relationship, whether it's romantic or business. When I go into a meeting with clients, I always think, 'I'm going to find a way to help this person.'

It may not be through me. I may not be in a position to help them, so it could be about referring them to someone else. It might be that we stay in touch, and I give them something to work on to grow and develop for later.

It's really about going into that relationship without feeling like I'm going to 'catch them.' I'm there to listen to them paint a picture of where they're at, and if it's in line with what I do, then I'll offer a solution.

I'm saying, "I'm here to listen, I'm here to help in any way I can. But I'm not going to try and catch you as a client."

The thing is, they're going to convince themselves that they want to be your client. You don't have to convince them, I think that's the positioning I've kind of come into.

It has even come to the point now where if a person says, "Yeah, I need to think about it," I'll reply, "Yeah, totally.

Awesome. What do you need to think about? How much time do you need to think about it? Who do you need to talk to first?"

I help them put together that plan, then I ask, "When should I follow up with you?" I've learned to kind of let go a little bit, in terms of not trying to hang on to that opportunity as much.

Learn to cultivate the opportunity. Do everything you can to nourish the soil and the water and give it a chance to grow, but at the end of the day, it has to grow on its own. You can't force it to.

This approach has come through in my outreach. I did a client video testimony with a client yesterday. One of the things she said was, "I really like your approach. It's like you're not trying to convince people of things, you're actually coming from that position of helping them. That's what comes through in the campaigns you do for me, and it's the way I like to do my business."

So, instead of trying to capture an opportunity, you must try to develop an opportunity by adding to the person's ideas, adding to their potential solutions. You're not trying to capture it in any way, you're trying to edify it. Edify the opportunity through listening, asking the right questions to develop the right plan, and then helping the client to develop their own plan. You will want them to come up with the idea, you're just asking the questions to help them come to their own conclusions. It's like being a cheerleader.

Once they come to their conclusions, whether they're saying, "I can't do this on my own" or "I can do this on my own," then I will start asking questions.

"What's your next step? What are you going to do? So you want me to hold you accountable to that?"

It's about coming from that angle of "I'm here to help you, whether it's directly or indirectly, I'm here to do that." and saying, "Okay, can I follow up with you in a couple of months and see how far you got in doing that?"

It's adopting a mindset like, 'Either I'm going to help you get through this, or I'm going to be your cheerleader.' I think that coming into conversations with that approach is awesome.

If, down the road, they say, "I don't need a cheerleader," that's fine too. At least I did my part in that I was willing to be there for them. It's not very often that I have that, it's usually like "Thanks for following me along my journey. It's been going great."

I really like the idea of taking the things we see and figuring out where the echoes and rhymes in nature are.

You can often draw a lot of rhymes from people and relationships. Over time, when you know enough about a certain topic, you start to recognize the rhymes around you in different ways.

I've really come to understand people pretty well over time, and I've been able to start to see what those rhymes are. I've found that nature can also further enhance this. It's like, "I'm struggling with something, but what I'm observing here in nature actually helps me overcome this obstacle when it comes to people."

People are complex creatures, but they have very simple needs. You can understand those simple needs and how to approach those needs in a way that follows the laws of nature.

If we start to follow the same laws of nature in our relationships as well, then we'll quickly realize that, although people are complex, we can understand their simple needs and come up with profound solutions. In essence, people don't have to be as complicated as we make them out to be.

We've covered some of those laws of nature in terms of observations and principles. If you come away with any understanding from this book, it should be knowing that your work won't be as hard if you can learn to observe those laws.

I'm hoping nature is a way of teaching those principles in a different light, so that it helps them stick in your mind a bit more. Being able to tell my story in the hopes of locking those ideas in your mind has been my main goal with this book.

It's saying, "Let's teach principles that have been taught, but not quite learned, because they haven't been taught in the right way or format."

I hope you gain a new way of looking at human relationships, and a new way of looking at human relationships through nature's lens, from this book.

It's about realizing that things are much bigger than you. And when you look at something much bigger than you, you no longer have to shoulder the full burden of it either.

I hope people get more curious. I hope readers will begin to feel like they don't understand things to their fullest extent and allow in some humility to look at new opportunities and go beyond, and sometimes re-look at things in a new light.

I hope this book gives you a refreshing view with which to look at relationships in a naturalistic sort of light that creates a fresh perspective that'll help lock those principles in your mind. That's my hope.

Life isn't necessarily about living, it's about connecting with people and the life around us. Our bodies and our minds are meant to connect with other people. I think if we can make connecting our main goal in life, then our life will be well-lived.

I often get focused on the idea that life is meant for living. Living is the by-product of connecting with people. That's true life.

Focus all your development and your process on connecting with people at a deeper level than you're connecting with them today. Use the tools that we talked about; curiosity, asking questions, and being able to develop the right questions to ask.

You know you're connecting with a person when they start to say, "You get me" or "I really like your approach." They'll tell you that. You'll start to know through the things they say.

The underscore is that life is meant to connect, it's not meant to live.

I find that I don't have to work as hard when I listen harder at the start of a relationship with a client. The harder I listen, the less I have to work later on.

If I really listen to what they're saying, and I listen to what I'm hearing in terms of my network and what they're doing, then I start to understand how to act. Once I understand how to act, I'll act in the right way.

My work has flourished because I've learned to connect with people.

For example, when I started working with one of my first VA's, I connected with her by asking, "How do you want to grow? How do you want your business to grow? Not necessarily just my business, but how do you want yours to grow?"

It's about learning to connect with everyone in your business, not only your clients, but your employees. Through connecting with them, you discover ways to empower them as well.

Now, my former VA is a business owner, just like me. She's got staff, and rather than her being my employee, I'm her client. But that only came about through me asking her questions about what she really wanted, not assuming I knew what she wanted.

I think that's the biggest thing in business. Don't ever assume you know what someone wants until you ask them. Until you dig deeper, sometimes they won't tell you initially. You might have to ask them more follow-up questions until you really know.

This positions you to be in a place where the person understands, 'This person is not out for their own best interests, they're out there for mine.'

Most of the value in my business comes from people understanding that I'm out to genuinely help them. They realize I'm willing to put in the time to listen and provide them with feedback, and in turn, they choose to become my clients.

Learn to challenge your own paradigms about people, and that can only be done by getting outside yourself. Networking works really well for being able to get outside of your paradigm because people can observe and share their observations from the outside.

When you think you've connected with a person, go deeper. Because deeper connections provide deeper, long-lasting solutions.

The deeper you go, the more long-lasting solutions you can provide and the more long-lasting relationships you can create.

Conclusion

T hose who approach the world with relentless curiosity are uniquely equipped to lead a more purposeful existence.

As a society, we have long marveled at the beauty and diversity of our world, yet we often find ourselves trapped in a cycle of self-absorption and overlook the vast potential around us.

It seems that, despite the fascination we have for our surroundings, we often get lost in our own thoughts and overcomplicate our own existence.

We become so focused and caught up in ourselves that we risk losing our curiosity and becoming disconnected from our own environment.

We become trapped in a self-centered mindset that distracts us from our true purpose, which is to experience, create and cultivate relationships and gain a better understanding of why we are here.

As a species, it is our duty to engage with our world and to turn over the rocks that hide its mysteries. However, our daily preoccupations often draw us into a narrow tunnel of self-centrism.

To tap into the wonders of the world requires the willingness to transcend beyond our self-centered concerns and venture out into the unknown, pushing the limits of our knowledge and opening ourselves up to boundless possibilities.

When we experience the weight of the world on our shoulders, it is often because we're not making enough connections. It means we have lost sight of the interconnectedness of all things, be it through human relationships or the natural world.

By building a network of diverse individuals and exchanging ideas with them, we not only challenge our existing beliefs, but also discover new ways to expand our creative horizons.

Recently, I had the opportunity to engage with an executive coach who specializes in Instagram, even though one might consider her a competitor of mine in a way.

However, I was curious about her methods and asked to chat with her. We eventually ended up talking for two hours, and we're now collaborating on a podcast to compare LinkedIn with Instagram, sharing our perspectives and learning from each other's experiences.

To truly flourish in life, we must be willing to take risks, challenge our assumptions and step out of our comfort zone. This means continually seeking out new connec-tions, exploring new ideas, and embracing the unknown.

Let others draw you into new possibilities.

Genuine connections between people are at the heart of any successful business. But to foster these connec-tions, we must be able to connect with ourselves first. This means embracing our own curiosity and recognizing that everyone we encounter has a unique story to tell.

Approaching each person as an individual with their own unique story to share allows us to tap into a deep well of human existence. By asking thoughtful questions and actively listening to the answers, we can start to under-stand the world from another person's perspective. In doing so, we not only deepen our connections with others but also expand our own understanding of the world.

It can be easy to get caught up in the idea of individual success, but it's important to remember that we are all connected. By recognizing and valuing the stories of those around us, we create a more meaningful and ful-filling life for ourselves and those we interact with.

I always find it helpful to remind myself that I need people around me, even though I sometimes get carried away with the idea of doing my own thing.

Connecting with others is the key to success, and it doesn't require going overboard. Learning to connect is the most significant aspect of it all. It involves creating bonds with nature, building relationships, and connect-ing your plans, visions, and goals.

This is just the starting point for connecting human nature with the natural world. There are many other connections to be explored, and these connections are essential to making the most out of the life we're given, whether it means rediscovering the wonder of it or preventing it from slipping away.

When I invite people over, if they've never held a snake before, or they're terrified of them, my biggest joy is to see them come away with a different outlook on the creatures.

I never force them to change their perception, but rather, I let them convince themselves. That usually comes through encouraging them to touch or hold a snake, and then they say, "Oh, they're not so bad after all!"

I believe this same principle applies to sharing any new idea. My secret is to ignite curiosity because once people are in that state of mind, they become more receptive. On the other hand, if they're not curious enough, then that door is closed, and it's okay to let the idea go and move on.

To effectively share an idea requires effective communication that hinges on our ability to spark curiosity in our audience. Without this initial flicker of interest, gaining access to their attention will be challenging.

To truly capture someone's attention, we must offer something that piques their interest and tugs at their curiosity. The only way to do that is to break free from routines and familiar environments and venture into uncharted territory, taking risks that may initially feel uncomfortable.

Even in my own life, working from home, I sometimes go days without stepping outside. I sense the effect it has on me, but I don't act on it. Yet when I take a walk, even around the block, I am suddenly reminded of my surroundings, and it's like a revelation.

I believe that one of the most critical mistakes in many sales approaches is the absence of curiosity. I can't stress this enough, curiosity is pivotal in the sales process because you need to get to a point where you admit that you don't know everything you thought you did about people.

This realization opens up space for understanding and comprehension.

As I said in the last chapter, I only read enough of a potential client's profile to spark my curiosity before an initial call. I avoid going in too deep until I meet the person because I want curiosity to fuel the conversation, not just my intentions.

At the heart of every engaging and worthwhile conversation lies a sense of curiosity.

It is through this sense of wonder and exploration that we discover what truly fascinates us, and we learn how to sustain that fascination over time.

Curiosity also has the power to transform our interactions with others, allowing us to become genuinely interested in their unique perspectives. Rather than just wanting to steer a conversation in a particular direction or convince someone of something, you should listen to them intently and ask thoughtful questions.

This approach not only enhances the quality of your conversations but also helps you build meaningful connections with others.

When you're genuinely curious about someone and what's important to them, the conversation transforms, and traditional sales techniques become irrelevant.

Approaching a conversation from a place of genuine curiosity and interest has the power to create a strong and lasting connection with others. When we take the time to truly understand their perspectives and experiences, we are better equipped to articulate our own position in a way that is both compelling and respectful.

When a person recognizes you're trying to comprehend their situation, as opposed to simply trying to push your point across, they are more willing to open up and share.

At the core of grace lies a fundamental sense of humility, a recognition that we are all part of something larger than ourselves and that there is always more to learn and discover about the world around us.

My family taught me the first lessons of grace. When I was younger, my siblings became my friends when I had none. That experience showed me what grace looked like in action.

Empathy is another crucial aspect of grace.

My earliest memory of practicing empathy was with ants. I discovered that they too experience pain, and that realization kick-started my journey toward understanding and empathizing with other people's pain.

In my business, I strive to identify people's pain points and address them. Instead of avoiding those conversations, I've learned to lean into them.

Doing so has allowed grace to flourish in my life, and I've witnessed the positive impact it has had on others. When you understand people's pain, you can create solutions, and in turn, build a business you can be proud of.

Learning to embrace those difficult conversations and actively seeking out people's pain points has been instrumental in cultivating grace in my life.

I believe intelligence is not just a matter of intellectual power, but also a willingness to explore and appreciate the richness and diversity of human experience. Every person has a unique story, a distinctive set of experiences, and a singular perspective on the world. Seeking out that unique perspective is what I consider intelligence.

This is particularly important when working with clients, especially in a saturated market of coaches. I do that with clients often. After working together, you start to get an understanding of how they're different from other coaches and other people. So I've learned to seek out that unique perspective. Drawing that difference out has been such a key, pivotal thing in this market.

When there are so many coaches offering the same things, how do you set yourself apart? That's where the unique experiences and knowledge that you've gained in your life come in.

I once worked with a coach whose daughter had cancer, and he spent six months in the hospital caring for her. That experience made him unique, and the knowledge he gained through that experience set him up to help others who have gone through similar situations. By recognizing his intelligence, we were able to reach out to senior leaders who have had a similar experience of cancer in their lives or families.

Ultimately, intelligence is shaped by our unique experiences and perspectives. Drawing out the unique intelligence in others begins with curiosity. It requires an open mind and a willingness to learn from those around us.

I have always been naturally curious, and although sometimes it has gotten me into trouble, I always encourage it.

For me, that curiosity began at a young age with my fascination with ants and their complex society. I saw a world that others often overlooked, and that ignited my interest. That was the initial spark that ignited my life-long passion for learning.

When I started out, I was curious about how things worked, and I began to piece together my understanding of the natural world and beyond. But as I learned more, I was always amazed at how much I still didn't know.

Nature was the catalyst that fueled my curiosity, but for others, it might be something entirely different.

It could be that they love getting out and working with vehicles, or they get curious about their body in terms of what it's capable of doing. Everyone has those first sparks.

Once curiosity ignites, it starts to cross-pollinate. And in my case, I began to see how things I observed in nature and related to people.

My curiosity about people was ignited when I went on my mission to Germany. That experience taught me how to connect with people and work in different environments, even those that made me uncomfortable.

I was learning to find comfort in discomfort, and curiosity kept me stable through it all. Every day, I learned something new about people, and it helped me understand why they react to things the way they do. Learning to get to that level with people takes the sting out of life a bit more.

In business, I think discontent fueled my curiosity.

I knew I was not content when I was working at the bank, most likely because I possessed enough knowledge to recognize that there were better opportunities out there.

I felt that there was something superior to what I was doing, and though I did not know what it was, I decided to start searching for it. Once I made a decision to explore, I began to notice opportunities that I had not seen before.

The real catalyst for my transformation came when I began surrounding myself with others who had different thoughts and ideas from my own. Being among

people with different perspectives allowed me to visualize the possibilities beyond my current ways of thinking.

Discontent gave way to curiosity, which led to connections and, ultimately, opportunity. These factors paved the way for where I am today.

At present, I find myself more content and curious than ever before. People often believe that they must be busy and do a load of different things to achieve their goals. While staying busy is important, it should be the output, not the input.

If we maintain a sense of curiosity, we will always be occupied with meaningful tasks. However, if we are merely busy for the sake of being busy, we will not progress toward our objectives.

We must allow a sense of awe and wonder to drive us forward.

Some people might say that we should avoid becoming too comfortable. I think that may be true to some extent; I believe I am not yet where I want to be, and I will never be until I die.

But I am surrounded by the people, opportunities, and experiences that truly intrigue me. Being around enough great people have made me realize that there is still so much more for me to learn.

We're surrounded by nature for a reason.

It's a learning ground. It's there to liven up our senses and teach us valuable insights. We must remain open to learning from the creatures, people, and natural elements that surround us.

These experiences can help us grasp higher concepts beyond our current understanding. We will soon realize that the more we think we know, the more we realize we don't.

Nature is a magnificent testament to the wonder and beauty of the world we live in. We are fortunate and privileged to be witnesses to its awe-inspiring display.

As such, we should look to nature as a starting point to learn and grow, to appreciate the world around us, and to focus on what is important for ourselves and future generations.

As human nature and nature itself are almost indistinguishable, we must also take the time to observe and learn from the people around us.

By embracing empathy and compassion, we can build meaningful connections with others. It is our duty to step outside of ourselves and foster a sense of community that prioritizes the well-being of all its members.

As a child, my grandmother would take me out for nature walks, which played a huge part in sparking my curiosity and appreciation for the natural world. She would often stop and encourage me to take a moment to appreciate the beauty around us.

This taught me the importance of taking a step back and appreciating the present moment. By cultivating mindfulness and being fully present, we can fully immerse in the beauty of our surroundings and find peace in the midst of chaos.

Take a tactical pause as often as possible, especially when life becomes overwhelming. By making this a habit, we can cultivate mindfulness.

The more mindful we can be of those around us, the more we can build meaningful relationships that enrich our lives and give us a sense of purpose.

My grandpa's last words, "Take care of the little guy," were a testament to how he taught me the importance of empathy and compassion and how useful it is in our lives.

For me, the words "Never let knowledge override your curiosity" or "Don't let what you think you know override what you don't" are equally important. It's easy to fall into the trap of thinking we know everything, but in reality, there is always more to learn.

So, never think you know enough.

I remember at my cousin's funeral, one of the themes was about making decisions on how we fill our days.

My cousin's brother invited him to go to the hot springs one day, but he had work and other obligations. However, he thought to himself, 'Will I remember this day with my brother in ten years? Probably. Will I remember the work I did today? No.'

So he went to the hot springs, and he later said, "I'm so glad that I did that."

I think my funeral will involve discussions of my undying curiosity about animals and insects and my love for them.

I hope that people will remember me as someone who took the time to stop and appreciate the small things in life, not just the big achievements.

In this book, I explore the idea of connecting with the virtues of nature and human nature, and how ultimately, what matters most is touching the lives of others.

By living virtuously, we invite virtue into our own lives and can positively impact those around us through our actions and experiences. It's easy to get caught up in the pursuit of material possessions and personal achievements, but true happiness and fulfillment come from recognizing and appreciating the abundance of life.

Despite the many challenges and difficulties we face, we are surrounded by countless blessings, and it is important to cultivate a sense of gratitude for them.

I think my unique perspective is that we've been given so much in this life. We are surrounded by so many amazing things that we're kind of spoiled in that respect. But somehow, we kind of miss that along the way, and we forget about what we have been given.

Gratitude is the art of appreciating what surrounds us, and for me, it is a foundational principle that can elevate our experience of life.

In this book, I strive to impress upon you, my readers, the significance of this quality, and how it can imbue one's existence with a richer depth and structure.

Learn to be grateful for the ground we stand on.

We often overlook the gifts that are right in front of us, and instead, fixate on what we lack.

But if we can learn to turn our attention to notice the beauty beneath our feet, we will open ourselves up to a vast universe of wonder and awe. If we can appreciate the blessings bestowed upon us and help others to appreciate them too, we can forge deeper connections with one another based on our sense of shared reverence for the world around us.

As a seasoned observer of both the natural world and the cut-throat business world, my hope for this book is to inspire readers to appreciate the interconnectedness between these seemingly disparate spheres.

By nurturing the gifts we have been given, regardless of our circumstances, and taking risks to explore and widen our horizons, we can live a more fulfilling and meaningful life.

While my story is unique to me, I believe that each individual has their own story, waiting to be uncovered and celebrated. Only by taking the time to truly understand ourselves and those around us can we unlock the true potential of our lives.

I invite you to join me in this pursuit.

About the Author

After climbing the ladder in the banking world for nearly two decades, Tyson Knauf quit his executive position to found his company, Knauf Solutions, which prides itself on working with executive coaches to significantly grow their businesses. His work with entrepreneurs, coaches, and business owners has led to great monetary success for his clients and incredible relationships in the process.

Tyson spends his free time and his work time in pursuit of grace and clients, as well as caring for his animals, his family, and the people around him.

He calls Fort MacLeod, Alberta, Canada home.

Find out more about Tyson at
www.knaufsolutions.com

www.ingramcontent.com/pod-product-compliance
Lightning Source LLC
Chambersburg PA
CBHW041144230326
41599CB00039BA/7169